ELAINE ROSIER   1994

COLLINS
PHOTOGRAPHER'S
HANDBOOK

COLLINS
PHOTOGRAPHER'S
HANDBOOK

MICHAEL FREEMAN

HarperCollins*Publishers*

First published in 1993 by
HarperCollins Publishers

Reprinted 1994

This book was created exclusively for
HarperCollins Publishers by Nigel Osborne
Design: Sally Stockwell
Editor: Judy Martin

For HarperCollins Publishers
Commissioning Editor: Polly Powell
Project Editor: Barbara Dixon
Art Editor: Caroline Hill

**A catalogue record for this book is available from
the British Library**

ISBN 0 00 412826 5

Typeset by Midford Limited, London
Colour reproduction in Hong Kong
Printed and bound in the UK

The author and publishers gratefully acknowledge the
assistance of **Leeds Photovisual Limited,**
20-26 The Brunswick Centre, Bernard Street,
London WC1N 1AE, and **Nikon UK Limited,** Nikon House,
380 Richmond Road, Kingston upon Thames,
Surrey KT2 5PR

CONTENTS

The essentials of photography are not exactly what you might be led to believe from looking at the advertising for cameras. As the equipment becomes more and more sophisticated, it sometimes seems as if there is a device for everything, and that all you need is the right camera, lens or gadget to produce startling, creative images.

Of course, this is not true, but there are some very useful new inventions in photography, such as automatic metering that allows for different compositions, and auto-focus. This makes it difficult to judge equipment with a sense of proportion. Although a camera makes photographs, it is incapable of making decisions. The nearest that an electronic camera comes to doing this is when the manufacturer feeds into its memory information about how other photographers compose and expose pictures (this is the basis of multi-pattern metering). All equipment has to be used with a sense of purpose. Some of it is essential, some of it can genuinely help you and some of it is no more than a

distracting gimmick. The only way of deciding what fits into which category is first to have a very clear idea in your own mind of the images you want to make – of what are, for you, the particular ingredients of a good photograph.

This is the aim of this handbook: to concentrate on the real essentials and to deal with the equipment as it deserves, as the set of tools for taking the photographs that start in the photographer's mind and eye. To this end, the book starts with the skills you need for making confident images – partly camera-handling techniques, partly graphic skills, looks at the special qualities of colour and light in photography; and continues with the entire range of subjects, from people to aerial views. All of this is essentially practical advice, but ultimately the success of any photograph depends on your judgement – on your eye for a picture. This book is not an operating manual for photographic equipment – it is an operating manual for the entire process of making photographs.

Framing the image The viewfinder frame is the most important part of a camera. Making a photograph is no more complicated than placing this black rectangular frame over any part of the scene in front of you, but the secret of a satisfying picture is often a matter of getting the framing just right.

With a single subject there are all kinds of choices: you can move the frame around, make it larger by moving closer or switching to a telephoto. Each different choice gives a new sense to the subject. If it fills the frame, the visual impact can be immediately striking; if small and isolated, the subject is set firmly in its surroundings. First decide which would work best for the scene in front of you. Filling the frame lets you show more detail in a subject, creates impact and cuts out irrelevant surroundings. On the other hand, the setting may be very important – it may be unusual, or put the subject in context, or simply help to make an interesting design.

▲▶ *Direction and impact An interior subject more than fills the frame: slanted lines increase our sense of being inside this palatial setting (above). In a tunnel of trees (top right), the cart at the corner of the frame draws the eye through the image and stresses movement away from the viewer. The gaze of its handler helps focus attention on the falcon (centre right), which forms the main subject of interest although placed far to one side. An extreme close-up of the face of a Buddha (right) gives immediate, unusual impact.*

Supposing that you choose to show the background, you can then usually place the subject anywhere in the frame. Each position makes the whole photograph work in a different way. Place a running man near the edge and he will either be moving into or out of the picture depending on his direction. Position a small figure near one corner, and the background takes on a new and interesting role. Avoid the obvious: aiming the camera like a gun to place the subject in the bullseye centre is often the dullest idea of all.

The majority of pictures have a main focus of interest that you will have to place somewhere in the frame. Decide exactly what this is and consider moving in towards or further away from the subject. When you are really close, it becomes a matter of simply fitting the subject into the frame. Sometimes, closing right in on just a part of the subject makes a strong image, but beware of just clipping the edges – this usually looks like a mistake.

◀ *Movement The judge has been placed at the left so that he steps into the picture. The framing anticipates the movement (left).*

▼ *Closing in The subject (below) is the dress inspection of a Greek Evzone. The deliberately tight cropping highlights just the essentials.*

▲ *Adding interest An ornate mirror hanging in a theatrical dressing room provided a solution to the otherwise uninteresting setting. With the help of a wide-angle lens to extend the depth of field from the frame to the people reflected in the mirror, the scene is neatly enclosed, and the baroque frame matches the period costume.*

► *Unifying the image Using the shade, trunk and branches of a tree gives extra depth to this view of a small-town church in Ontario. It is also a solution to a design problem – the background and sky of the conventional view were very ordinary, and bringing the setting to the foreground tied the picture together more successfully.*

Graphic framing Occasionally you can find – or make – a kind of frame within the scene you are photographing. It might be something as obvious as an archway or the overhanging branch of a tree, or it might be more inventive – an arrangement that exists only because of the way you position the camera. In any case, the pre-requisite is that one element in the foreground surrounds at least a part of the view beyond. Like any strong technique, it succeeds when used sparingly and with originality. If repeated often, or made too obvious, it becomes a cliché.

When it does work, it gives a graphic completeness to a picture. This is partly because the frame is natural – being part of the scene itself, and not just an arbitrary rectangle like the camera's viewfinder. There is a kind of formality in the way it contains the view.

Another reason why the natural frame integrates a photograph is because the frame makes a distinct foreground. Combined with the scene beyond, this gives a sense of depth, and helps to pull viewers into the picture, giving them the impression that they are looking through from one scene to another.

Experiment with the size of the frame you have found within the given elements of your subject – in relation to the picture frame in the viewfinder. If you leave too much space between the two, the framing effect will be lost. If there is only a narrow gap between them, this itself can make an interesting shape. Silhouetted frames, such as you can find when looking outside from a darkened interior, are graphically the strongest of all.

Points and lines Quite apart from what a photograph is about, the image is made up of points, lines and shapes, and these create their own effect on the eye. When they are obvious and definite, you can use them to strengthen the design and to direct attention to different parts of the picture.

In photographs, points occur when subjects are very small in the frame, and contrast with their setting. A white yacht against dark water seen from a distance is one obvious example, or a lone figure walking on a skyline, or a scattering of peppercorns on a kitchen surface. Always place a single point with care: it affects the entire proportions of the picture.

Lines can be distinct, like the edges of a building, or made up of a string of points, such as a line of parked cars in the distance. The angles of the lines – and how many there are – have an effect on the feeling of a picture. Horizontal lines, for instance, often give a solid, stable composition. Vertical lines tend to be more dynamic than horizontals; they have an in-built sense of movement, usually upwards. Be careful to align both horizontals and verticals exactly – they are always compared with the edges of the frame, and if they are slightly out of true, the mistake is obvious. Diagonals are the most dynamic of all lines, with a strong sense of movement and direction. You can use them to bring liveliness to even a static view like a still-life. Create them by tilting the camera or choosing a specific viewpoint. Curved lines also bring movement, but of a smooth, flowing kind; you cannot create these in the viewfinder, they have to be in the view from the start.

▶ *Adding emphasis Two graphic devices were used to tie the picture of the umbrellas together – the eye-line of the girl and the position of her arm. Placing her at the top right produces a strong diagonal down to bottom left.*

HINTS & TIPS

Faces always draw attention in a picture, and the eyes more than anything else, so much so that when we look at a photograph of a person, we tend to follow the direction of their gaze. In a picture this implied line is known as an 'eye-line'. You can use this effect to put movement and direction into the image.

◀ *Receding lines* Curving diagonal lines that converge in the distance give a powerful sense of direction and movement – entirely appropriate to a view of an urban freeway (left). The means were straightforward: using an extreme wide-angle lens (20mm) from a high viewpoint (a footbridge), angled sharply downwards.

▼ *A sense of design* (below) A low viewpoint through a wide-angle lens makes the most of the curves of the BMW building in Munich, in a deliberately abstract treatment. The lower concave curve counters the convex ones above.

Shapes After points and lines, shapes are the other important graphic element in photographs. Although there seems to be no limit to the variety, only definite, obvious shapes really count in an image. There are just three basic shapes – rectangle, triangle and circle – and all others are variations. If you use shapes well, they will help to organize your images. Mainly, this is a matter of recognizing them and then framing the view to emphasize them. Shapes, like lines, can alter the mood of a photograph. Rectangles tend to look solid, sober, and very ordered – squares most of all. A lot of this has to do with matching the shape of the picture frame. Compositions with rectangles can look very precise and cubist.

Triangles occur through the viewfinder in all kinds of ways. Three strong points or subjects, for instance, make a triangle inside the frame, and this is often an effective way of arranging a small group portrait. A strong perspective view, particularly with a wide-angle lens, makes a kind of triangle – looking down a long, straight road, for example. Tilting the camera upwards, so that tall subjects like buildings or trees seem to slant away from you, can have the same sort of effect. What makes triangular composition so useful in a photograph is that it combines the liveliness of diagonal lines with the clear organization of a simple shape.

▲ *Triangle* The man's head forms the apex of a well-defined triangle, with a solid base in the bicycle cropped to fill the frame.

▲ *Square* The repeated squares within the vertical format rectangle create an orderly composition, though set to one side.

Circles occur less often, and can be attractive precisely because they are not so common in photographs. Any circular composition really concentrates the image, and pushes attention to the centre. Full-frame fish-eye lenses (see page 51) create a circular feeling to a picture.

Remember that all these effects have to work inside the rectangular frame of the picture. This means that they interact with the edges and the corners, and you can use this to strengthen the image. You could, for example, align an edge or a corner of something in the picture with the frame, or intersect diagonal lines with one edge.

Apart from finding and using shapes and lines to organize or enliven a photograph, you can sometimes use them to influence the way in which other people will look at an image. Diagonals and curves in particular create a sense of movement and direction. If you incorporate them with care, you can encourage the eye to move along them from one part of a picture to another. One reason for doing this might be that an important part of the photograph might appear unavoidably small, and you want to make sure that it is not missed. You could use a line to 'point' to it: eye-lines can also be used in this way. In fact, pictures are sometimes more interesting when they take a little time to be appreciated.

▲ *Rectangle The lines of the receding pillars create rectangles of diminishing size that echo the overall format.*

▲ *Circle The natural silhouetting of this architectural detail provides both a strong focal point and a frame within the frame.*

HINTS & TIPS

Don't underestimate the eye's ability to find balance in a picture. For example, with one small object way off-centre against a fairly even background, the 'empty' area acquires its own visual weight, so we see a kind of balance.

▲ **Symmetry and balance** *A close symmetrical composition of a leaf gives an enclosed, concentrated feeling (top left).*

The other two photographs are more graphically active in the relationship between the off-centred subjects and their settings.

Symmetry and asymmetry The different parts of a picture always have some kind of relationship with each other, even if you don't plan it that way. The most basic relationship is balance. In a picture this works in much the same way as it does in the real world, and you can think of the various parts of a picture – shapes, points, colours, tones, and so on – as having 'visual weight'. Anything that stands out naturally against its background has more of this 'weight', and dark areas tend to be 'heavier' than light ones.

Imagine the picture frame as a kind of scale, balanced on a point in the middle. One subject, right in the centre, is obviously balanced, as are two similar ones on either side (such as the faces of two people talking). One subject in a corner of the frame seems to tip the balance. In a simple image, with just one or two obvious points of interest, it is easy to see how they work, but in busier images the relationships can be more complex.

There are two kinds of balance – static and dynamic. Symmetrical compositions – with everything centred and ordered – are perfectly balanced but static. They have a kind of solid, geometrical appeal as long as you compose them exactly around the centre, although this can be boring. What they usually lack is movement – they don't invite the eye to wander around the frame.

▲ *Positioning The curve of regularly hung buckets at the top of the frame mixes symmetry and asymmetry, with outward movement at the sides.*

▲ *Dynamic tension A wide-angle lens exaggerates the outward flow of the side walls in the University of Virginia. The curves pull attention out from the centre.*

Some of the most effective symmetrical photographs work on a slight element of surprise – surprise that the photographer found symmetry in a view, or a graphic surprise such as the lines converging strongly.

The other type of balance is dynamic and asymmetrical. A classic example is one strong small point in a corner of the picture offset by a larger but weaker shape on the other side. This creates interesting visual tension.

Proportions Most pictures are divided in some way, deliberately or not. Lines make the most obvious dividers, or blocks of tone or colour, and if they are obvious, it is worth giving some thought to the proportions. In some kinds of photography where you need to work quickly or intuitively, such as reportage, there is precious little time to experiment, but in others, like still-life, you can change viewpoint and even move the subject to make adjustments.

You can divide the frame in any number of ways and proportions, the more easily if your subject has strong, definite lines and shapes. There are no absolute rules, but some proportions are more generally pleasing and easy to look at than others. Like balance, dividing a picture frame involves the idea of harmony. You can ignore it or go against it for deliberate effect, but you can also use it to help make the design of the picture more satisfying.

Most of the ideas on frame proportions come from painting, but photographers usually work intuitively. One of the easiest techniques is to make major divisions (up-down, left-right) roughly a third of the way into the frame. This works particularly well in 35mm photography, because the viewfinder frame is itself in these proportions – 2:3. A more sophisticated method is the Golden Section, the best known 'harmonious' division. It is based on ratios (the ratio of the smaller part to the larger part is the same as that of the larger part to the whole frame), but in practice, it is fairly close to dividing by thirds. The point where the up-down and left-right divisions cross also makes quite a good place to position a single subject.

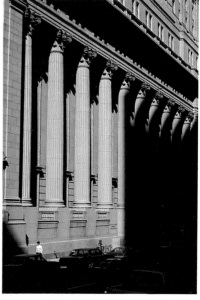

▲ *Fine cut Most of the frame above is taken up with a San Francisco mural, but for scale and setting, a small slice at the left takes in a group of passers-by.*

▶ *Light and shade The play of light on this building in Toronto makes a neat division (right). A telephoto lens was used to crop in tightly.*

PLACING THE HORIZON

In landscapes and many other long shots, the horizon line insists on making its own division of the picture, and the more the contrast between sky and land, the more strongly it cuts through the photograph. The horizon also tends to overwhelm the composition when it is flat (and so lines up with the top and bottom edges of the frame), and when the view is bare and very simple.

Depending on the actual view, you can place the horizon line at any height in the frame, from close to the top to right at the bottom. The two most conventional positions are roughly a third of the way down or a third up, and much depends on whether the landscape or the sky is more interesting. The extreme positions – at the top or bottom – can be more exciting, but need a justification. If the horizon is very close to the top, it concentrates attention on the very narrow band of sky – good with a distant stormy sky, for example. If very low in the frame, it gives the sky overwhelming prominence – good if there are interesting clouds, and to give the impression of wide open spaces. In all cases, make sure that you keep it level – an angled horizon line is hard to ignore and spoils a picture.

A final choice that you have is to break the horizon line – by changing your viewpoint so that part of the foreground comes more strongly into view. In a landscape, for instance, lowering the camera position may make a rock or plants appear higher in the frame.

▲ *Alternative compositions*
A central horizon (top) creates an even balance that needs to be enlivened by strong shapes within the picture. Asymmetrical divisions are more spacious, emphasizing sky (above centre) or foreground (above). The less of the sky you see, the more you are drawn into the landscape.

Finding the angle Many people simply shoot what they first see from where they first see it. This is by no means always the lazy option – photography is often about catching the immediate on film, and there may just not be enough time to move around before shooting. When there is time, use it to make sure that you have the best viewpoint for the shot. Sometimes this may be no more than a matter of improving slightly on your first position, but you may find that a radical change gives you a picture you had not imagined existed. When photographing landscapes, or a building, or a still life, walk around and try out the possibilities.

Keep in mind your different focal lengths. Viewpoint and lens are inextricably linked, and with unusual viewpoints – from above and below – wide-angle and telephoto lenses give completely different types of image, even more so than from ground-level.

A strongly angled upward view, of something like a building from its base, can give an unusual and powerfully graphic composition. With a wide-angle lens the vertical lines converge strongly; with a telephoto, details are foreshortened. In both cases, because the view is a little strange, take care over the framing – your subject may end up being scarcely recognizable.

Views from above often make the most interesting alternative treatments. There is a built-in appeal to bird's-eye views that has to do with being able to see over things – the privileged view. Look out for bridges, balconies, viewing platforms on the top of high-rise public buildings and towers.

▶ *Finding the unexpected view*
Deliberately organized for a strong graphic impact, this vertical shot of a man checking stock in a jeans factory was taken from a balcony overhead. From this angle, not only is the view unusual, but the quantity of jeans appears more impressive than from a conventional viewpoint.

HINTS & TIPS

Use the roof of a car for extra height. If you need to make a slow exposure using a tripod, there is less risk of camera shake if you use the delayed-action timer and climb down off the car.

▲ *Height* An upward angle emphasizes the man's view of this Burmese stupa (above).

▼ *Detail* A tall ladder gives a close view of the subject within the setting (below).

◀ **Waiting for the shot** (left)
In this photograph of farmers winnowing rice, timing is the key to the shape and rhythm. The repetitive action gave plenty of time to wait for the right combination of figures.

▶ **Continuous action**
Catching the stream of visitors passing through a doorway in Beijing's Forbidden City (right) involved waiting with camera in place for an interesting pose.

▲ TIMING

Anticipating the shot Almost every scene in front of a camera changes, sometimes so slowly that you can't notice just by looking, sometimes so quickly that only a fast shutter speed can capture it. Landscapes change because of the light and the weather; scenes with people change with every movement and gesture. Quite apart from technical questions like the shutter speed needed to freeze a particular moment, timing affects the composition.

This is most obvious if you are photographing people in action, such as in a reportage situation. If someone is walking across your view, say from left to right, then the direction itself becomes part of the photograph. If you frame the shot so that they are on the left of the frame, then they are walking into the frame and this leads the eye into it also. If you place them on the right, they will be moving out of the scene, and this may draw attention away from the rest of the picture. Changes in gesture and stance may create shapes that are more interesting at one moment than another.

The key to all this is anticipation – having an idea of what will happen next and how it will look through the viewfinder. This is easier if the action is repeated, such as someone working and doing the same thing over and over again. Then you can afford to take your time and decide exactly which split-second makes the best-looking image. Experiment with viewpoint as well – certain movements look better from one angle than another. In a slow-moving scene, such as a view over countryside with clouds passing, use the same technique. Decide how a cloud or a patch of sunlight in a particular position affects the composition, and change the frame for that; if necessary, wait until the next occasion.

Finally, don't become too concerned about missing a moment that you think has gone forever. Of course, this does happen sometimes, but there is no single 'best moment' in any situation.

HINTS & TIPS

If you have an attractive view and want to add human interest – say, a passer-by walking through – compose the shot as it will look, not as it does in its 'empty' state. Human figures catch the eye more than most subjects, so allow for this extra visual weight.

▲ *Immediacy* The timing of the shot of a diver doing a flip (top right) needed a fast reaction to capture the disjointed combination of a flipper and the painted buoy.

▲ *Selection* At New York's Rockefeller Centre (above), the overall scene is static, but the figures moving inside it alter the pattern subtly. Timing in this case meant waiting for an appropriate arrangement.

Rectangular formats The 35mm format rules photography today. By far the majority of cameras bought and used are 35mm, and its 2:3 proportions set the picture frame for most photographs. Not only this, but the frame is usually horizontal – a direct result of the way cameras are designed. In practice, this rarely causes any difficulties. A large part of photography has to do with fitting a scene into the space that the viewfinder allows you.

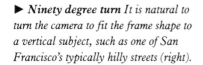
▲ *Appropriate format In many landscapes, like this view of a Spanish village (above), the 35mm frame matches the sequence of horizontal lines that are a normal result of perspective.*

▶ *Ninety degree turn It is natural to turn the camera to fit the frame shape to a vertical subject, such as one of San Francisco's typically hilly streets (right).*

Because our natural binocular view of things is horizontal, a 35mm frame used horizontally gives good image proportions for most views, and is quite easy to use. Nevertheless, there are other options – different frame shapes – and making use of them broadens your creative choice.

The most simple and obvious variation with 35mm format is that the camera can always be turned on its side for a vertical view: hardly breath-taking, but surprisingly little done. As a vertical frame, a 35mm photograph is slightly less easy to view, and the eye naturally tends to fall to the lower half of the picture – often the most comfortable place to position a subject. A vertical frame is often worth the slight extra effort to think about and shoot, if only to bring some variety to your pictures. And, many subjects simply suit a vertical composition – a full-length human figure standing, for example. With non-vertical subjects, it is usually more natural and comfortable to place them lower than the centre of the frame – you can then use the unoccupied upper part to show something of the setting.

Other camera formats and special designs employ a variety of frame shapes. Medium-format cameras using roll film produce 4.5 x 6 cm, 6 x 6 cm, 6 x 7 cm and 6 x 9 cm images. Panoramic cameras frame scenes in stretched proportions that are 1:3 or even longer. Large-format cameras typically frame images in 4:5 proportion. However, you don't need to feel restricted to the particular film format of your camera.

◀ *Formal design A square frame, photographed with a 6 × 6cm roll-film camera, perfectly suits this geometric upward view of a decorated ceiling. A longer frame shape could have been made to work, but the precision and formality of the ceiling called for the most straightforward treatment possible.*

While most photographers work by preference to the viewfinder frame they have been given, you always have the option of cropping the picture area. There are a number of ways of doing this. If you make prints of your photographs, simply adjust the bars of the printing frame and move the enlarger head up or down until the image is sized the way you want it (if you have prints made for you by a photo-finishing lab, make a sketch or trace of the image to show how it should be cropped).

A horizontal frame is easy to look at, because our binocular vision gives us a side-to-side view of things. In long views, like landscapes, the scene is most often laid out horizontally, and so suits the 35mm, 2:3 format well. Square frames, the classic medium-format shape, are actually more suited to cropping than making interesting compositions (though there are many exceptions). One problem is that a square is so rigid and formal that it encourages very symmetrical and centred images. Patterns and textures, however, often work very well in a square frame, simply because it doesn't have a bias one way or another. If you do your own printing, a square negative has some advantage in allowing you to crop horizontally or vertically.

Panoramic frames are possibly the most interesting of all, and don't necessarily need a special camera – you can crop an ordinary horizontal frame when printing or even for projecting a slide. They are dealt with in more detail on the next two pages.

▲▶ *Suitable subjects* Both views, in the classic proportions of 1:3, were taken with a purpose-built panoramic camera. Broad landscapes with low relief suit this format very well – eliminating much of the foreground and sky, the panorama concentrates attention on the details of the landscape and emphasizes its sweep.

The widest view A number of cameras, even 35mm, are made specially to produce wide, panoramic views. Even with a normal camera, modern slow and medium-speed film is so fine-grained that there are no problems with cropping an image down to a panoramic shape. But why go to the trouble? The reason is that, seen from the right distance, such a wide frame comes very close to a realistic view of the world as we normally see it. As well as seeing life through a vaguely horizontal shape (see page 24), we look at things by scanning – usually from side to side.

Panoramic frames normally have between 1:2 and 1:4 proportions, and such a long format, trimmed top and bottom, gives the eye a chance to roam around the picture. Provided that you stand close enough to a panoramic photograph (especially if it is a large print), you can't take in everything at a single glance. Instead, you discover different things within the picture, even if this takes only a few seconds. This alone draws people into a panorama, and helps to make it more interactive than a normal image. It helps if you can include plenty of detail or events in the frame, so that the eye has every opportunity to explore.

▶ **PANORAMAS**

A panoramic frame is surprisingly easy to use for composition. Even if the scene itself doesn't seem to be so horizontal, the frame can act like a storyboard, with things going on in different parts. It even works to have the frame 'divided' into panel-like areas.

A panoramic camera is ideal but expensive. You can crop a normal frame in the following ways: by setting the frames of the printing easel to a 1:3 (or thereabouts) shape if you print yourself; by marking this shape on the selected frame of a contact print if you send negatives or prints out to a lab for printing; or by sandwiching a strip of black card or black film rebate with a slide in its mount if you use a slide projector. Or, simply shoot a panoramic scene in different sections and paste the prints together later (make sure that you overlap the images when you shoot so as not to leave any gaps).

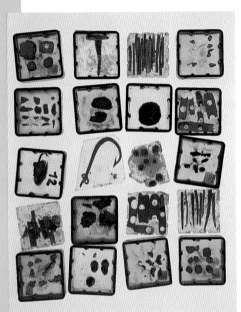

◀ **Like objects** *Small archaeological artefacts embeddded in blocks of resin (left) were arranged in a back-lit still life to emphasize their similarity – but with some deliberate angling for interest.*

▼ **Variation** *In a similar set-up for cut rubies (below), two larger stones were introduced to provide a focus of attention, placed slightly off centre.*

PATTERNS

Order and mass Patterns work by repetition – a kind of wallpaper effect, if you like. To make an interesting photograph of a pattern in a man-made design – floor tiles, friezes and so on – you need to be a little inventive. Simply photographing a pattern that someone else has carefully worked out is likely to make a very unsurprising image.

Patterns abound in nature, but many of the more unusual ones are small-scale or large-scale. Use close-up photography (see pages 150-3) to discover the patterns of leaf veins or scales on a butterfly's wing. A high viewpoint such as a mountain overlook can show patterns in a river bed, or fields, or rock formations. To isolate pattern areas, a telephoto lens is often more useful than a wide-angle. With man-made objects, masses of things make some of the best pattern pictures.

▶ **Cropping in the camera** *Soldiers on parade form an obvious pattern that, like the view of yachts (top opposite), is usually handled best by a telephoto lens. The long focal length makes it easy to crop in tightly on the group, and so exclude the background and foreground that have nothing to do with the pattern.*

▲ *Massing* A long telephoto lens (400mm) converts a mass of yachts in Marseilles harbour into a pattern by compressing the perspective (above). The foreshortening renders them all the same size and this helps the sense of pattern.

▶ *Selective framing* A window display of votive pieces on sale in a Greek shop (right) allows cropping in at a choice of scales.

HINTS & TIPS

Patterns work most effectively in a photograph if they 'bleed' off the edges of the frame. Move in close enough, or adjust the lens focal length, so that the pattern more than covers the picture area – it will then look as if it continues much further.

Camera technology The main difference between the various types of camera is the format of film that they accommodate. By far the most popular is the 35mm format, designed to take the standard sprocketed film that gives an image 24mm wide and 36mm long. Despite the small film size, image quality is good enough for almost any use, including quite big enlargements. Because of their popularity, 35mm cameras and film receive a lot of attention from manufacturers, and are constantly improved: the introduction of automated functions has increased the choice across the range of 35mm models.

Medium and large-format cameras are less likely to be used by non-professional photographers for reasons of practicality – cameras in the smaller 35mm format are more available, easily portable and convenient to use – and because they are significantly higher-priced. However, they have specific functions and the main advantage of the larger formats is improved image quality.

In addition, the technology of cameras is changing once again with the new generation of electronic cameras linked to computer and video facilities for storing and viewing images. Offering also vast potential for different approaches to image-manipulation and quality control, this has yet to become a fully realized and accessible photographic medium, but it points to a future containing new standards for image-making.

Auto-focus compact non-reflex

35mm non-reflex These cameras have a viewfinder that is separate from the lens, the traditional design. Older models with manual focus carried the disadvantage that the photographer had to focus the image without seeing exactly what the camera saw. Non-reflex cameras therefore became less attractive for serious photography when single-lens reflex cameras with through-the-lens viewing were invented, although they have always had a considerable popular value as convenient 'snapshot' cameras.

Now, however, with auto-focus and viewfinders linked to auto-zoom lenses, that problem is largely overcome, and the great advantage of non-reflex cameras is that they are compact and easy to use. The most basic, least expensive models are auto-focus compacts. Auto-focus is now almost universal in compact cameras – only the very cheapest

Auto-focus zoom compact non-reflex

feature simple manual focusing in steps. The lens is usually 35mm for maximum use, although a few models have two lenses – normal and wider-angle.

The auto-focus zoom compact has the more sophisticated feature of automatic zoom. This would have been impractical formerly in a non-reflex because of the disparity in focus between viewfinder and lens, but auto-focus makes the zoom function efficient. The range of focal lengths is typically around 38-105mm. Different models provide special features, such as pop-up flash, variable flash modes, or remote control.

There is just one professional contender in this category, the redoubtable Leica, the first 35mm camera ever designed. It is tough and very well made, has interchangeable lenses, and some later models feature automatic functions. The quality of the Leica translates, however, into a much higher price. If you are choosing a 35mm non-reflex for serious photography it is worth also noting that many professionals now use top-of-the-line compacts as unobtrusive or back-up cameras.

Professional non-reflex

Basic manual focus SLR

35mm single-lens reflex (SLR) These cameras show the view through the lens, via a retractable mirror and a pentaprism that flips the image right way round. The big advantage of through-the-lens viewing is that what you see is what you get. Basic manual-focus models are deliberately simple, lacking sophisticated electronics, and they are sturdy and very reliable. Metering is usually centre-weighted (see pages 44-45) and manually controlled.

Programmed manual-focus SLRs contain more electronics that give a choice of metering modes, as compared to the basic manual-focus models in which you adjust both the aperture and the shutter speed to match the display. Programming can be geared to aperture priority or shutter priority; for example, with shutter speed priority you choose one speed which remains a fixed setting, and the aperture is varied automatically

Professional manual-focus SLR

to achieve the required exposure. There are programmes that favour high speeds, slow speeds or depth of field, and often a choice of metering method. Professional manual-focus cameras are top-of-the-line models built to be extremely reliable and to the highest quality – but they lack the benefit of auto-focus and are only partly automated.

Basic auto-focus SLRs compare in simplicity of use with auto-focus

Auto-focus SLR

compact 35mm non-reflex types. They have the extra facilities of interchangeable lenses and, in many models, a built-in, often pop-up flash. The most advanced and expensive SLRs are the professional auto-focus models, made to the highest specifications. These are the flagship cameras of the few manufacturers who compete at this level of equipment. The 'professional' aspect includes strong construction, highly efficient automated functions and also manual over-ride facilities for exceptions to the rules.

Long telephoto lenses, which cover only a tiny angle of view, are only practical with 35mm SLR cameras, as is close-up photography.

Roll-film cameras These cameras, also known as medium-format, use film that is 6cm wide, and their main claim for attention is better image quality than 35mm. Indeed, the frame shape in this size of film that corresponds to the proportions of a 35mm slide or negative is more than five times larger, although there is considerable variety in the formats. For example, roll-film is ideally suited to a panoramic frame (see pages 26-27), since it is able to give large-format image quality in this extended frame shape. The principal frame proportions of panoramic formats are 6 x 12cm and 6 x 17cm.

Partly because the film size is large enough to allow cropping, and partly because the market for these cameras is fairly small and specialized, there are very few standardized designs. There are few inexpensive roll-film cameras, and the top models are spectacularly expensive.

Medium-format non-reflex

Non-reflex cameras Although most roll-film cameras are reflex, there are a few non-reflex models that have the practical advantage of being physically lighter than SLRs. Some have a retractable lens that also makes the most of their relative compactness. They use a simple rangefinder which overcomes the problem of focusing inherent in non-reflex cameras by displaying images as seen through both the viewfinder and camera lens; when the two images coincide exactly, the focus is correct. The standard for formats in most rangefinder roll-film cameras is between 6 x 6cm and 6 x 9cm.

The 645 format is space-saving, because it uses the film width as the longer side of the frame – a questionable restriction, given that the important feature of roll-film cameras is image size. However, the 4.5 x 6cm format is almost three times the size of a 35mm frame, and there are some compact camera models not much larger than their 35mm counterparts.

645 format non-reflex

Medium-format SLRs What are essentially the same mechanisms that are contained within the 35mm SLRs take up much more space in the medium-format roll-film cameras. They do not have as standard the pentaprism used in 35mm SLRs to put the image right way round into an eye-level viewfinder. Waist-level viewing, looking down on the viewfinder, is the traditional design for medium-format SLR models. However, it is generally possible to fit a pentaprism viewer to convert the camera's operation to eye-level viewing. Most models are based to some degree on the Hasselblad, a pioneering design of its day and still the doyen of roll-film cameras. Reflex viewing allows interchangeable film backs: a maximum size of 6 x 7cm gives greater flexibility than 6 x 6cm. The full range of lens focal lengths is available for all models in this category. By comparison with 35mm SLRs, these cameras are not highly automated.

Waist-level SLR

The Pentax 6 x 7 is a unique design – that is, unique for a roll-film camera. It is purpose-made for eye-level viewing, and is essentially a scaled-up version of a basic 35mm design. In this lies one possible drawback, as the design does not incorporate interchangeable backs. But for the more generous format, this is a camera that handles quite quickly and easily, particularly suited to hand-held shooting. Compared to 35mm SLRs the handling technique is different: your free hand, the one not operating the controls, plays a more supportive role for the camera's base and lens.

Eye-level SLR

The 645 format SLR has an image size that is markedly smaller at 4.5 x 6cm, but the camera designs are among the most advanced. The format provides an additional choice in the middle of the range between 35mm and the larger formats available from roll film. In some models, the electronic input and automated features are close to the level found in 35mm SLRs. Those which have hand-grips and an eye-level viewfinder fitted as standard are relatively fast and convenient.

645 eye-level SLR

Twin-lens reflex (TLR) This very old-fashioned style of roll-film camera still persists, mainly because of price and reliability. The two lenses aligned vertically have identical focal lengths. The upper lens is for viewing, the lower for transmitting the image to the film – an unwieldy arrangement, but not at all complicated. Viewing is normally at waist-level, although there are some models that permit an eye-level viewfinder to be used. When the image is projected upwards onto a viewing screen as in waist-level viewing, it has a two-dimensional quality that gives a good sense of the way the photograph itself will appear.

Twin-lens reflex

CAMERA TYPES ▶

Field camera

Large-format cameras

View cameras, as they are known, use sheet film, which is available in a number of sizes. Most commonly used formats are 4 x 5in (10 x 12.5cm) and 8 x 10in (20 x 25cm). The entire reason for using these very bulky, ungainly cameras is to get the best possible image quality. You can most easily appreciate this in an exhibition print or an extreme enlargement such as a poster. The largest negatives can be printed without an enlarger – in a contact printing frame – with extraordinarily fine results.

Compared to the sophisticated automation and rapid action of modern 35mm SLRs, view cameras are the product of a completely different age. In principle, they have changed little since the early days of photography and require a very much modified pace of work. But there are distinct advantages in the control you can have over composition of the image in the camera. Camera movements – shifts, tilts and swings – are features of large-format cameras that make it possible to keep verticals straight, distort shapes and tilt the focus to almost any angle you choose.

Field cameras are light and fold up compactly, but the lightness can be a disadvantage working outdoors. Technical cameras, which derive from field models, are sturdier and more technically advanced, but their movements are restricted. Mono-rail cameras are designed mainly for studio use, and resemble laboratory bench equipment. Modular, adaptable and extremely versatile, they are ideal for precision photography.

Mono-rail camera

Digital camera

Electronic cameras This new class of camera records images onto an electronic medium, such as a disk. This is the future in photography, but for now the problem is resolution – the image quality. Electronic cameras must match the standard set by fine-grain film, while still being used hand-held. Available prototypes are not yet near that point.

The Canon ION is a still-video camera that can store up to 50 high-band pictures on each removable 2-inch floppy disk (or 25 at higher resolution). The image pick-up is a charge-coupled device (CCD) that can record nearly half-a-million pixels. Images look very good on a monitor, but make only moderate prints. They can be viewed on a television with a high-band still video player: to see them and work with them on a computer they must first be digitized.

Digital cameras also record on CCD and store on disk, but the results can be loaded into a computer immediately. The Kodak Professional Digital Camera System is based on a Nikon F3 body, but in place of the film back has a 1.3 million-pixel CCD. It can shoot in colour at the equivalent of film speeds from ISO 200 to ISO 1600; in black-and-white from ISO 400 to ISO 3200. Up to 600 images can be stored on a 200MB hard disk in the (bulky) storage and preview unit. Images look good on screen and in small prints, but do not match the resolution of film.

Holding the camera Treat the camera as a craftsman's tool. The steadier you hold it and the more familiar and adept you are with the controls, the more picture possibilities you will be able to seize – and with fewer mistakes. The difference between a steady and an unsteady grip can be as much as three f-stops. In other words, if you are particularly good at holding the camera still, you can use slower shutter speeds than normally. This alone extends your range of shooting, to poorly lit interiors and a little later into the evening. A few simple techniques will ensure that you avoid camera shake in any normal shooting, while everyone can improve their lowest reliable shutter speed by practising. Aim to be able to hand-hold a 35mm camera with a 35mm lens at $^1/_{30}$ sec.

The slowest hand-held speed also depends on the lens you use. Camera shake is worse with a telephoto than a standard lens because the magnification is greater. The easiest lenses for hand-held shooting are wide-angle – a small tremor hardly affects the picture at all.

▲ *A steady position To obtain a clean shot, your body needs to be well balanced. For a low viewpoint you can kneel, sit or* *lie, but try to eliminate tensions that may cause unnecessary movement. Steady the camera in a firm, two-handed grip.*

As well as steadiness, quick access to the controls is vital. A split-second may make the difference between a good shot and nothing at all. Exactly which controls are important varies from camera to camera, and automation helps a lot. With manual-focus, you must have one hand on the focusing ring almost all the time; with an auto-focus camera there is no need. Become completely familiar with the workings of your camera so you can react without having to think about procedures.

Shoulder bags Unless you use just one camera with one lens, a shoulder bag is an essential part of the equipment. In fact, even carrying the minimum, you will still need to add film and items such as spare batteries, notebook, filters and flash. A shoulder bag should above all be comfortable to carry and easy to work from. The size is critical – spacious enough to hold everything you are likely to need for a particular trip or assignment, but not so big that it weighs you down when full, or becomes loose and floppy with only a few things in it. Resist the temptation to stuff it with more than will be useful – a shoulder bag is a working piece of equipment. For transporting cameras, a hard case is likely to be more useful (see also pages 156-157).

You can have a carrying bag made to your own specifications, or even use an ordinary bag not specially designed for cameras. Tough waterproof fabrics are widely used for proprietary makes of bag, often lined and padded. Leather wears well, and the longer the bag is used, the more comfortably it fits the contours of the body. Lined canvas is extremely tough, and waterproof, although heavy. Look for a broad shoulder strap running underneath the bag, interior padding or compartments, and easy access.

Tripods For all the inconvenience of carrying them and setting them up, tripods are indispensable for low-light and slow shutter speed shots, and have hidden advantages in composition. Before buying a tripod, try out your camera on it, with the heaviest lens you are likely to use. As a simple test, with the camera secure and the tripod head tightened up, tap the end of the lens as you look through the viewfinder. If you see the frame move much, you need a stronger tripod. Tripod heads are an important, separate choice. Again, go for strengths. Pan-and-tilt heads have separate movements for each axis, which means that you can make small adjustments without affecting others. Ball-and-socket heads have a single lock for all movement, which makes them quick to use but not quite so easy for fine adjustments.

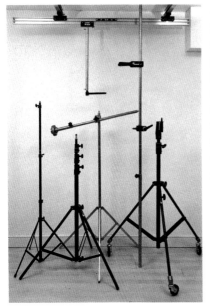

◄ *Tripods These provide different features in basic design and attachments. The length of both tripod legs and adjustable centre column dictate maximum height (remember that narrowing the base or increasing the column height reduces stability). A side-bar attachment that enables the camera to be mounted clear of the legs is helpful if you are shooting downward.*

HINTS & TIPS

If you are shooting at the edge of reliability – say with a shutter speed of ¹/₃₀ sec without a tripod – use more film than you would normally. You can expect one or two frames to be spoilt by camera shake.

EXPOSURE

Controlling the light Exposure is the amount of light that reaches the film. Too much and the photograph will be pale and washed-out; too little and the image will be dark and murky. The ideal is usually just enough to make a picture in which you can see all the important detail, and which has a good range of tones and saturated colours. All of this depends on the sensitivity of the film – a slow film needs more light than a fast emulsion. The job of measuring the light and working out the exposure is given to a light meter, nowadays normally built in to the camera. You can work out the exposure for yourself, but it is much easier to rely on an automatic camera to do it for you. Only when the scene is lit strangely, or when you deliberately want an unusual effect, would you really need to over-ride the automatic meter.

Cameras control the exposure in two ways: with the shutter and the lens aperture. The shutter delivers a dose of light, short or long according to its setting. The aperture, which is a multi-bladed diaphragm set in the lens barrel, cuts down the light when it is closed down. In an automatic camera, these mechanisms are linked to the metering system – this measures the light entering the camera from the scene, and sets the exposure accordingly.

Depending on the automatic model, you can choose the aperture and the camera sets the shutter speed (aperture priority), or you can choose the shutter speed and the camera sets the aperture (shutter priority), or the camera can choose both according to pre-set rules (program metering).

HINTS & TIPS

If your camera meter fails, follow this rule of thumb: on a sunny day set the aperture to f16 and the shutter to roughly the same number as the speed of the film you are using. So, if you have ISO 100 film in the camera, shoot at $1/125$ sec at f16. You can adapt this by varying aperture and shutter by the same number of steps – for example, $1/500$ sec at f8 (two stops less light from the shutter, two stops more light through the aperture). Add one more stop if the light is hazy, up to four if overcast.

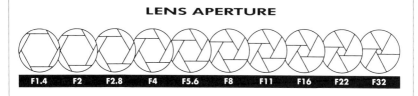

LENS APERTURE

| F1.4 | F2 | F2.8 | F4 | F5.6 | F8 | F11 | F16 | F22 | F32 |

The size of the lens aperture is measured in f-stops, and the reason for using this special notation is that the same numbers can be given to all kinds of lenses. Each f-number refers to the same amount of light passing through to the film, whatever the lens. For example, f4 on a 35mm lens is actually a smaller aperture than it is on a 200mm telephoto because of the different optics, but the exposure will be exactly the same. The sequence of f-stops looks strange because the numbers are the ratio of the aperture to the focal length, but each stop passes half the light of the one preceding it, in the sequence shown.

Setting shutter and aperture yourself To make exposure settings easier with a non-automatic camera, both the shutter and aperture controls are stepped in the same way. Each step, identified by a click as you move the controls, doubles the exposure in one direction and halves it in the other. As you increase the shutter speed, in fractions of a second, each change means that the shutter moves twice as fast. If you open up the aperture, each click means that twice as much light can enter.

The simplicity of this arrangement is that you can operate the shutter and aperture in tandem – if you need to use a faster shutter speed without changing the exposure, all that you need to do is open up the aperture by the same number of steps. Say you are shooting at $^1/_{60}$ sec and f 5.6 and want a faster speed to deal with a quickly moving subject. Turn the shutter speed dial two steps to $^1/_{250}$ sec, and the aperture two steps to f 2.8 – the exposure stays exactly the same.

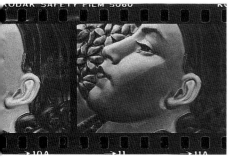

◀ *Bracketing This means making additional exposures lighter and darker than the metered reading. A bracket of three is: + $^1/_2$ stop, normal, – $^1/_2$ stop. A bracket of five would be: + 1 stop, + $^1/_2$ stop, normal, – $^1/_2$ stop, – 1 stop. It uses up more film than usual, but is useful insurance for an important shot on colour slide film. With negative films, bracketing in 1-stop steps is usually enough.*

EXPOSURE

Reading the exposure As exposure is so well automated now in most cameras, it is hard to make a serious mistake. Nevertheless, some images will fool most meters; and some photographers have special preferences for lighter or darker versions of a scene. It is important to become familiar with the way your meter works in different lighting situations. The table below shows typical variations – ideally, you should try them all and check how your meter responds.

BASIC EXPOSURE SITUATIONS

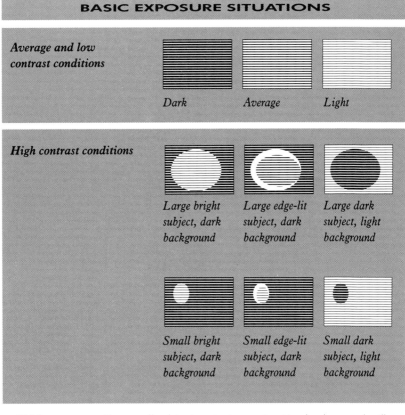

Average and low contrast conditions

    Dark   *Average*   *Light*

High contrast conditions

Large bright subject, dark background   *Large edge-lit subject, dark background*   *Large dark subject, light background*

Small bright subject, dark background   *Small edge-lit subject, dark background*   *Small dark subject, light background*

While a scene with a small subject against a contrasting background will mislead ordinary averaging meters, the new generation of 'smart' meters, using the segmented system, can usually recognize what is needed. In these, the frame is divided into a number of segments, and the value of the lighting in each segment is read separately. The resulting pattern within the frame is then compared with a number of types of photograph that have been programmed into the system's memory. If the meter matches your image to one of these known types, the exposure should be near-perfect.

If you have a more basic metering system, such as average or centre-weighted, it is important that you see the view as your meter does. In the average system, the meter reads the entire frame with no bias, and calculates the average. (Average systems are now less commonly used than previously.) A centre-weighted meter reads the entire frame, but gives more emphasis to the centre of the frame, where most people place the subject, and very little to the top, which is often filled with sky.

If a scene has an average mix of brightness – and most do – then trust the camera's meter. If most of the picture is brighter or darker than average, you will have to override the meter. Otherwise, an automatic metering system will turn a largely white scene, such as a snowscape, into a grey photograph. It will do the same with a view in which a small, spotlit subject stands against a dark, shadowed background. Using a spot meter, you can read just the important part of the picture, and lock onto that. Or, if you have time, move up close to take a reading of the key subject.

HAND-HELD METERS

Spot meters measure a circle with an angle of view of usually 1°, although many modern cameras are just as effective in spot metering mode. The most useful feature of normal hand-held meters is the incident-light reading, by which you can measure the light that falls on the subject, irrespective of how dark or bright the subject and background are. This kind of meter is heavily used in studios, and for this reason most hand-held meters are also flash meters that can read short pulses as well as continuous light.

Incident reading

Direct reading

Skin tone reading

Grey card reading

White card reading

Meter readings
An incident reading measures illumination, a direct reading records light reflected. Substitute readings from skin or card also measure reflected light.

Shutter speed The camera shutter is one way of controlling the dose of light that reaches the film – the other is the lens aperture. It also controls the way movement looks in the photograph. The conventional treatment is to ensure that the action is captured sharply and clearly, by matching the shutter speed to the movement – too slow, and some of the picture will be blurred; too fast, and you must either use a very wide aperture (and so little depth of field) or a faster film.

The frozen image With very fast action, such as in athletics, some of the movement may be too fast for the eye to register, and the appeal of a photograph that catches something happening in mid-action is that the view is new and a little unexpected. What is important here is not how fast the action really is, but how fast it appears to be in the viewfinder. Fast movement at a distance, or seen through a wide-angle lens, makes quite a slow-moving image. The table opposite shows the slowest shutter speeds likely to freeze some common subjects if they fill the frame. If the moving subject is smaller in the frame, a correspondingly slower speed will do.

► *Head-on movement In a predictable situation, choose the film speed to suit the light, shutter speed and aperture. A head-on shot such as this cavalry charge by the Carabinieri at the annual Palio in Siena can be made with a slower shutter speed than usual, but here ¹/₅₀₀ sec was the absolute minimum. In the late afternoon shade, with an f2.8 telephoto lens, the camera was loaded with ISO 200 film.*

Panning If you turn the camera to follow the action, this is called panning. It helps to freeze movement by slowing down the image and works best with a smoothly moving subject (such as a car rather than a runner) that crosses the view from one side to the other. As the table shows, panning allows you to use a slower shutter speed and still avoid blur.

Deliberate blur An effective way of getting across the impression of movement is sometimes to use a slow shutter speed. If most of the subject remains recognizable, the blurred parts will give a good sense of movement. If you pan with a slow speed – say ¹/₆₀ or ¹/₃₀ sec – you can get the subject sharp but the background streaked horizontally, helping to separate the two, as well as conveying speed. An extreme method is to use a very slow shutter speed, such as ¹/₂ or I sec, and move the camera as you shoot.

▲ *Slow shutter speed* In the photograph of a busy store (above), the camera was mounted on a high tripod and the shutter set for 1 second to show the movement of shoppers within range.

◄ *Changing motion* A Camargue cowboy swerves to avoid a bull (left). With the pace of the action uncertain, only ¹/₁₀₀₀ sec was a safe shutter speed.

Subject filling frame	CAMERA HELD STILL			CAMERA PANNED		
	◄ ►	◢◣	▲▼	◄ ►	◢◣	▲▼
Walking hand movements	¹/250	¹/125	¹/60	¹/125	¹/60	¹/60
Jogging, children playing	¹/500	¹/250	¹/125	¹/250	¹/125	¹/60
Running, dancing, city traffic	¹/1000	¹/500	¹/250	¹/500	¹/250	¹/125
Motorway traffic, tennis serve, racing cyclist, horse galloping	¹/2000+	¹/1000	¹/500	¹/1000	¹/500	¹/250

DEPTH OF FIELD

▲ *Restricted depth Shot with a medium telephoto, this image of tulips employs shallow depth of field to isolate a flower against a wash of colour.*

▲ *Front-to-back focus Good depth of field is essential to juxtapose different elements. A 180mm lens stopped down to f 32 needed a shutter speed of ¹/₁₅ sec.*

Location of focus Whatever you focus on is the sharpest part of the photograph. How much else appears sharp – in the foreground and the background – depends on the depth of field. There are various ways of measuring this, but as depth of field itself is not exact, appearance is the most important guide. If it looks sharp, it is sharp.

The depth of field in a picture depends on the size of the aperture and on how close the subject is. A small aperture improves it, and there are two ways of obtaining this – using a wide-angle rather than a telephoto lens, and shooting at a smaller f-stop. The difference that distance makes is that in close-up there is less depth of field. Good depth of field is one of the conventional ideals in photography – the better it is, the more detail. However, it pays to choose the depth of field whenever you can, because there are several advantages in limiting it. Front-to-back sharpness is not always the best idea. At its simplest, if you restrict the depth of field to just the main subject, this will usually help to make it stand out from the surroundings. This, though, is always more effective with a telephoto lens than with any shorter focal length.

> **HINTS & TIPS**
>
> *Brightly lit scenes show when the depth of field is shallow more easily than scenes under flat lighting. The more contrast in the picture, the more careful you should be if you want front-to-back sharpness.*

To check depth of field with an SLR camera, press the preview button. The view will darken if the aperture is small, but what you see is what you will get on film. At normal distances, you will get the best depth of field for whatever aperture you use if you focus one-third of the way into the picture. In close-up photography, focus half of the way in.

▲ *The effect of stopping down a telephoto lens on depth of field – in this sequence, from left to right, the camera was first focused on the nearest roof finial, wide open at f5.6. Then the focus was changed to the furthest finial, still at f5.6. Finally, it was set mid-way between the two points, and the lens stopped down to f32.*

Strong depth of field is usually good for:	Shallow depth of field is usually good for:
• Most views with a wide-angle lens • Sweeping landscapes • Architecture • Still-life • Record shots and copying	• Isolating a subject from cluttered surroundings • Concealing unwanted backgrounds • Improving the sense of depth • Making a wash of colour • Shooting through foreground obstructions

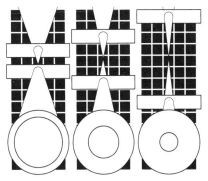

◄ *Aperture The cones in this diagram represent circles of light on either side of the camera's point of focus. The eye reads the narrowest part of the cone as in focus, with sharpness decreasing as the cone expands. At full aperture (far left), rapid expansion means that very little appears sharp; this is shallow depth of field. With the same lens stopped down, the focused area increases, and depth of field is greatest at minimum aperture.*

L E N S E S

Focal length The most important difference between lenses is focal length, which is only the distance in millimetres from the lens to the film, but it affects the angle of view. This changes the entire character of the image – and the way in which you use the camera. Short focal lengths give a wide angle of view, long focal lengths a narrow, magnified view. In the middle of the range is the standard lens, which has a focal length more or less the same as the corner-to-corner measurement of the picture frame. A choice of focal length is useful, either as interchangeable lenses or in the form of a zoom lens (see pages 54-55).

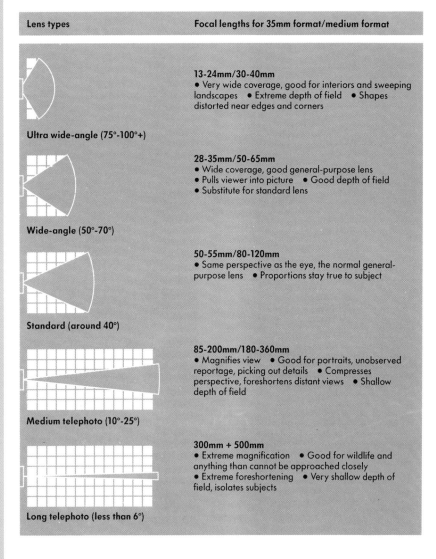

Lens types	Focal lengths for 35mm format/medium format

Ultra wide-angle (75°-100°+)

13-24mm/30-40mm
• Very wide coverage, good for interiors and sweeping landscapes • Extreme depth of field • Shapes distorted near edges and corners

Wide-angle (50°-70°)

28-35mm/50-65mm
• Wide coverage, good general-purpose lens
• Pulls viewer into picture • Good depth of field
• Substitute for standard lens

Standard (around 40°)

50-55mm/80-120mm
• Same perspective as the eye, the normal general-purpose lens • Proportions stay true to subject

Medium telephoto (10°-25°)

85-200mm/180-360mm
• Magnifies view • Good for portraits, unobserved reportage, picking out details • Compresses perspective, foreshortens distant views • Shallow depth of field

Long telephoto (less than 6°)

300mm + 500mm
• Extreme magnification • Good for wildlife and anything than cannot be approached closely
• Extreme foreshortening • Very shallow depth of field, isolates subjects

AUTO-FOCUS

▶ *Aiming for focus* Auto-focus systems read off a small area in the centre of the image. As long as some of the main subject is there (top right), the auto-focus is able to measure a degree of specific contrast in the central area, and so it works well. When the subject is off-centre (below right), the camera focuses only on the background, which is filling the inner frame that the auto-focus reads. However, the sharpness of this picture has been retained by locking the focus first on the right-hand figure, then realigning the camera to compose the shot with the figure to one side.

Auto-focus speeds up shooting, which is all to the good, and nearly always works the way you would like it to. But, like any other kind of automation, it follows rules, and if you take a photograph in not quite the way the manufacturer expected, the focusing may fail. Most auto-focus systems work by measuring the contrast between edges of things — high contrast means sharp, and servo-motors in the lens adjust the focus to suit. The area measured is small — a rectangle in the centre of the frame outlined in the viewfinder.

If you frame the shot so that the main subject is off-centred, the auto-focus will simply fix on the background. The same will happen if you shoot a close-up of two people on either side of the centre. The answer is to aim first at the subject that you want sharply focused, lock the auto-focus and re-frame the shot. A second occasional problem is that the system needs something to focus on — a blank wall provides no point of focus. If the auto-focus has difficulty locking, aim at something with more obvious detail.

The majority of new cameras now have auto-focus, but they are not all equally efficient. Apart from accuracy, there is a difference in how fast the system can lock on to a subject — the reaction speed. An auto-focus system should be at least as fast as you can be with a manually focused lens.

▶ **LENSES**

▲ *Limited distortion* *In this view of the Hearst mansion at San Simeon in California, the perspective effect of a 20mm lens pulls the lines of the swimming pool outwards with dynamic effect (above).*

◀ *Relative scale* *To show all the details of a food scientist making a gas analysis of packed food (left), a 20mm lens was stopped down to f22.*

Wide-angle lenses For 35mm cameras, any lens with a focal length shorter than 35mm is considered wide-angle (in fact, a 35mm lens just qualifies, but is also used by some photographers as a substitute for a standard lens). The outstanding feature of these lenses is, of course, that they cover more of a scene than usual, but they also have other, more subtle qualities. By compressing a wide angle of view onto the same size of film frame, they create a strong perspective that can give photographs a distinctive flavour. They also tend to draw the viewer into the picture.

In increasing effect, the usual focal lengths for 35mm cameras are: 35mm (mild), 28mm (the 'average' wide-angle), 24mm (strong), 20mm (very strong). Beyond these are some quite specialized lenses, expensive and often quite bulky, with focal lengths as short as 13mm. All of these are 'corrected', meaning that straight lines appear straight. A different kind of design, known as a fish-eye, produces even wider coverage at the cost of a circular distortion that bends lines near the edges of the frame. A true fish-eye makes a circular image inside the normal rectangular frame; a full-frame fish-eye covers the entire frame.

The most obvious use for a wide-angle lens is to cover a scene that you can not manage by moving further away with a standard lens: an interior, for example, or the sweep of a broad landscape from an overlook, or a crowd scene. However, the graphic effects of a wide-angle lens are usually more interesting. Lines and shapes are stretched towards the edges – and even more towards the corners – giving an exaggerated perspective. Diagonals become a strong part of wide-angle views, often converging towards the distance. You can use these to put energy into a photograph, but beware of distortion that simply looks odd – as a rule, avoid placing obvious shapes like circles or faces near the corners. Use the viewfinder to experiment with the composition, keeping it to your eye as you move around – a small change in the camera position will make a big difference to the image.

▲ **Fish-eye** *This shot of a carpet of autumn leaves, photographed with a 16mm full-frame fish-eye from only a few inches away, gives the typical curved distortion.*

HINTS & TIPS

To make a wide-angle lens work to its maximum effect, include both foreground and background, and shoot from close to the nearest objects. You can create strong, and sometimes surprising, relationships between the near and far parts of a scene.

LENSES

Telephoto lenses The direct opposite of wide-angle lenses, telephotos have long focal lengths and give a narrow angle of view. This narrow angle means that they enlarge a small part of the scene, and so are good for closing in on a subject without having to move nearer. Telephoto, in fact, is a design of lens that squeezes a long focal length into a shorter barrel – a 300mm lens, for example, measures less than that – but is almost universal. The other type of long focal length is a mirror lens, also called catadioptric, in which the light path is folded into a very short, stubby barrel.

Telephoto lenses are longer and heavier than other types. Fast telephotos – that is, with wide maximum apertures – need very large front elements, making them even bulkier. They need rather more care in use than shorter focal lengths: because they magnify, they are more prone to camera shake, and the longest ones are best used on a tripod.

Telephotos give a compressed perspective, which can make interesting compositions in which the planes of a scene are 'stacked'. It also makes distant objects – like the moon – seem much larger. By being able to pick out parts of a view, telephotos are good for isolating and emphasizing a single subject. Their depth of field is very shallow, which you can use to good effect – it helps subjects stand out against soft backgrounds.

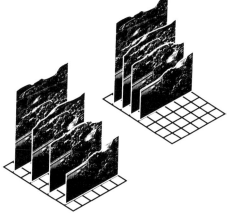

◄ *Layered images Telephoto lenses compress the view so that distant subjects can seem almost on top of nearer ones. Often, as in this view of a well-known switchback street in San Francisco, the different parts of a scene appear stacked in planes. The longer the focal length, the greater this effect – here a 400mm lens was used.*

◀ ***Moving in*** *The tight cropping of a telephoto used on this ship in a Montreal harbour reduces the sense of space around it and appears to pull the background closer. Long lenses are an essential tool for focusing attention on details (left).*

▼ ***Lens size and subject*** *The chart below shows the most suitable telephoto lenses to choose for particular subjects, and their advantages in use.*

SUBJECT	MOST USEFUL LENSES	FEATURES
Portrait	85-105mm	Better proportions to face than with standard lens.
Reportage street shots	135-180mm	Close views of people unobserved and full-figure across-the-street shots.
Landscapes	150-600mm	Medium telepoto for gently compressed views, long telephotos for picking out distant details.
Theatre, ballet	Fast 200mm	Close view from off-stage, wide aperture to cope with lighting conditions.
Sports	Fast 300-600mm	Close views from spectator lines, fast enough to freeze action (focal length depends on which sport).
Wildlife	300-600mm, preferably fast	Medium telephoto for stalking and large animals, long telephoto for everything else.

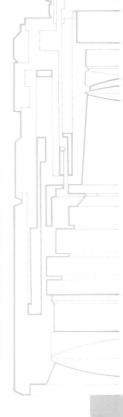

Cropping with a zoom Instead of using a set of lenses, each with a different focal length, you can use one or two zoom lenses to cover the same range. The only slight drawback of a zoom lens is that it is slightly heavier than one fixed lens and a little slower. On the other hand, a zoom lens gives the convenience of several focal lengths in one, which saves weight overall and allows you to move to another focal length in an instant. The ranges vary between makes: there are wide-angle zooms, mid-range zooms which span moderate wide-angle to medium-telephoto, telephoto zooms and ultra-telephoto zooms. Some highly automated cameras feature powered zoom.

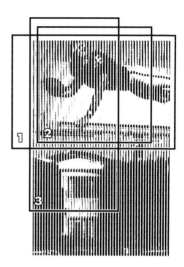

◀ *Framing the view A zoom lens with telephoto range offers a choice of framing, although often with greater similarity between the images than from a wide-angle zoom. This static scene of a billboard in Los Angeles benefits from precise composition and the cropping is fine-tuned.*

The zoom ratio is the difference between the shortest and longest focal length that the lens covers – and also the difference in angle of view. A 24-50mm zoom has a 1:2 ratio, a 75-300mm zoom has a 1:4 ratio. the bigger the ratio, the more choice you have, but the bulkier the lens is likely to be. Changing focal lengths with a zoom lens is rather different from the fixed-lens method of switching from, say, 28mm to 35mm. The range is continuous, so that you can fine-tune the composition by choosing any position between the two extremes. In a way, this is an on-the-spot version of cropping a slide or negative when making an enlargement. It often helps to start at the widest angle and then move in on a part of the image. Study the wide view and imagine where you could place a smaller rectangle. Don't limit the choice to a straight, centred zoom. Cropping an image will often take you away from the centre of the scene.

The only danger with this infinite choice is that it can slow the photography. If your subject allows you plenty of time to experiment, take the opportunity, but in faster situations, like reportage or sports, avoid fine adjustments. They may simply lose you a picture.

◀ ▼ *Alternative images* With a zoom lens set at its widest, imagine the different positions of smaller frames within the view. These are not usually best composed in a direct line to the middle of the scene – as you increase the focal length, the dynamics of the image change.

Negative and slide film There are three main kinds of camera film: colour negative, colour slide and black-and-white negative. In addition, there are many kinds of specialist film for doing particular jobs, such as making duplicates of slides, negatives from slides, copies of negatives, and so on. What you choose should depend on how you intend to use the photographs. Most amateurs choose colour negative film because the best quality prints can be made from it – a greater range of tones and colours is possible in a print made from a negative than in one made from a slide. Professionals shooting for gallery prints also normally use colour negative film – the print quality is higher, and it is easier to make corrections to colours and shading.

COLOUR FILM

Fine-grained   *Fast colour*   *Tungsten-balanced*   *Infra-red*

Most colour film processing has been standardized, even for different makes of film. The main colour slide process is known as E-6, and the main colour negative process C-41. Though less commonly used, a favourite of many professionals is the

K-14 process used exclusively for Kodachrome films – these are unusual in that there are no colour dyes in the film itself; instead, the colour is added during the complex process. Kodachrome images are very sharp and extremely stable.

On the other hand, slides last longer than colour negatives, and are easier to publish from. What you see is exactly what you get, without the need for any intermediate stage. A colour slide, whether you project it or view it on a light box, has more brilliance and intensity than a print ever can. High contrast scenes can cause problems, especially with colour slide film. In a view with very bright highlights and dark shadows, no exposure will work perfectly. As a rule, expose slide film for the highlights; if you are using negative film, expose for the shadows.

Whether you use colour negative or slide film, it is possible to make prints and slides from either. Using special film, you can make internegatives from slides and slides from negatives. If you have your photographs transferred into digital form so that you can display them and change them on a computer (see pages 160-165), most scanners can deal with either.

▲ *Film speed* Static subjects such as city architecture do not need the extra sensitivity of fast film, and benefit from slow film's finer grain (here ISO 50).

▲ **TYPES OF FILM**

Speed and grain Probably the most important difference between films is their speed. This is a shorthand way of referring to how sensitive they are to light: a slow film needs more exposure than a fast film to capture an image. As short exposures are much more convenient to make than long ones – no blur or camera shake with a fast shutter speed, and good depth of field from a small aperture – this would seem to give fast films all the advantages. However, there is more to it than that, as one of the effects of making a film faster is to make it more grainy. The best picture quality comes from films with small, tightly packed grains, and that means slow.

Many photographers use more than one speed of film at a time, so as to have the choice of top image quality when the conditions are right for a slow exposure, and shooting fast action or in dim light when image quality is not so important. You might, for example, want to shoot a landscape on slow film to record all the details and textures, while in street photography it is more important to be able to use a reasonably fast shutter speed.

Colour quality There are deliberate colour differences between makes of film; this particularly applies to slides. No colour film can give a perfect rendering of a scene, because there are only three layers to make up all colours and the dyes available have limitations. What is possible, however, is for manufacturers to make films that boost some colours and tone down others, according to what they think photographers will want. One of the most obvious differences is between the films made by the largest Japanese and American manufacturers. The Japanese films tend to have more heightened colours, which can be good or bad according to your taste. Use your own judgement in choosing between different makes of similar films. There is no single best treatment of colour, and in any case new films come onto the market all the time.

HINTS & TIPS

On colour slide film, colours look richer when they are darker rather than lighter. To increase colour saturation, try slight under-exposure by setting the camera's film speed selector 1/3 of a stop higher – for example, for an ISO 50 film, set the camera to ISO 64.

Colour balance Most colour films are made to be used in daylight in the sense that if you shoot in the middle of a sunny day, there will be no colour cast in the photograph – whites and greys will look white and grey. This is a matter of colour temperature (see pages 80-81), and daylight films are balanced for 5500 K. Flash units have the same colour as sunlight. A few colour films are balanced for tungsten lights – photographic ones, not domestic – at either 3400 K (Type A films) or 3200 K (Type B films). Apart from use in the studio or interiors with this kind of lighting, tungsten-balanced films have a special advantage in that they are made to have very little reciprocity failure (see below). So, you can reliably make very long exposures in daylight with a Type B film and an 85B filter.

COLOUR MIXING

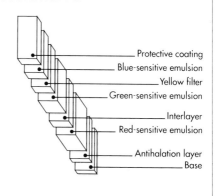

All the colours that we can see can be made by mixing blue, green and red light (essentially, the way our eyes work). Colour films take advantage of this by having three layers, each one sensitive to a different colour. When the film is processed, each layer is dyed with its colour, so that together they give the full range of colours when you project or view them.

Protective coating
Blue-sensitive emulsion
Yellow filter
Green-sensitive emulsion
Interlayer
Red-sensitive emulsion
Antihalation layer
Base

Professional vs. amateur Some films are available in two versions, professional and amateur. The difference, though never great, is that the professional films are selected to higher tolerances in qualities like colour balance and film speed. The normal manufacturing differences between batches, which can show up in a slight colour cast, are supposed to be absent. But they keep less well under ordinary conditions than amateur films, which tend to have a better colour balance after two or three months.

Special films There are also films made specially for such tasks as duplicating slides, making negatives from slides, and slides from negatives. Of the very few special films intended to be used for direct shooting, the most unusual is probably false-colour infra-red film. Designed for mainly scientific uses such as aerial photography to check healthy vegetation, its three emulsion layers are sensitive to infra-red, green and red instead of the normal blue, green and red.

Reciprocity failure If you shoot at a very slow shutter speed, most films behave a little differently from normal. Typically, the photograph will appear darker than you expect and, with colour film, there may be a colour shift as well. The exact effect is not easy to predict without testing, as each make and type of film behaves differently, and film manufacturers do not recommend slow speeds for their ordinary daylight films, so give few details.

▲ TYPES OF FILM

This loss of sensitivity is called reciprocity failure because the reciprocal way in which the aperture and shutter speed work together to control exposure gives up at very slow (and very high) speeds. Normally, halving the shutter speed from, say, $^1/_{60}$ sec to $^1/_{125}$ sec, and at the same time doubling the aperture, such as from f 8 to f 5.6, makes no change to the exposure. But at long exposures – a few seconds, for example – this no longer holds true. In practice, it doesn't make much difference with black-and-white films, because of their great latitude (see page 62). With colour film it is a problem, especially because the three colour layers suffer from this 'slowing' effect to differing amounts. Many colour slide films, but by no means all, turn green. The only answer is to test the films you normally use, and then buy a colour correction filter of the opposite colour.

(see page 62)

HINTS & TIPS

To change from one kind of film to another in mid-roll, do the following. Note how many frames you have shot and carefully rewind until you can just feel the leader come free of the spool (impossible on some cameras with only automatic re-wind). Remove the film and write the number of exposed frames on the leader with a marker.

Storing film Films are not completely stable, and change slowly with time. If you keep a film beyond the date recommended on the box it is likely to be slower, lose contrast, and if it is colour, lose its richness. Ideally, use film and have it processed soon after buying it. If not, be careful to store it cold and dry. Heat and humidity are film's worst enemies, and speed up its normal ageing. Conversely, dry refrigeration slows the ageing, and many professionals, who buy film in bulk, keep it in a refrigerator or freezer.

You can keep most films safely for several months in a refrigerator at about 40°F/4°C. For longer-term storage, use a freezer at around 0°F/-18°C. Be careful to allow time for it to warm up at room temperature before opening it, to avoid condensation – at least an hour for refrigerated film, three hours for frozen film. In both cases, store film in its unopened can or wrapper to keep it in its original dry condition.

Special processing If you shoot film normally – such as by relying on the camera's automatic metering – then normal processing will usually give you ideal results. In fact, for the best image quality (contrast, richness of colours, fine grain) the film needs to be processed for just the right time and at exactly the recommended temperature. Nevertheless, processing labs can increase or reduce development – at times this can help to improve an image; more often, it can salvage pictures after a mistake. Even film manufacturers now recognize that photographers find this useful, and some ultra-fast films are made specially for you to choose at what film speed you want to use them – these films usually have a 'P' in their name.

Increasing development is known as 'pushing', reducing is known as both 'pulling' and 'cutting'. In practice, this means making the film behave as if it had a different speed. You could take a roll of ISO 200 film, set the film speed indicator on the camera to ISO 400 (twice as fast), and then have the development pushed by one stop. If you made a mistake when shooting, this saves the images. Or, you may find yourself in lighting conditions too poor for shooting at a reasonable shutter speed with the only film you have. In that case, just up-rate the film and treat it as faster; mark it for push-processing when you have finished. Some professionals do this as a matter of course so that they need only carry one kind of film.

Altering the development affects the appearance of the image. The change in contrast can be useful if the scene you photographed had too much contrast or was too flat – but of course, any changes you make will affect the complete roll of film. Professionals shooting large-format sheet film can take advantage of this more easily, and pull or push the development of single shots. Push-processing by one-third or half a stop is useful for cleaning up large areas of white in an image. There are limits to how far the processing can be changed without ruining the image quality. These depend on the type of film, but are usually two stops in either direction.

EFFECTS OF PUSH AND PULL PROCESSING

Push processing
- Lets you use the film as if it were faster
- Increases contrast
- Weakens blacks
- Increases graininess
- Changes colour slightly (E-6 films: slightly redder)

Pull processing
- Makes film behave as if it were slower
- Lessens contrast
- Makes whites 'muddy'
- Changes colour slightly (E-6 films: slightly bluer)

Test developing For safety, after a long trip test a small part of the film before processing every roll. Do this either by having one roll from your batch processed first, or a few frames clipped from the end of a roll (this is known as a clip-test and available from some film processing labs as a special service at a small extra cost). Judge the results; if you have made any mistake in the exposure and the pictures look too dark or too light, have the lab push or pull the processing of the remaining rolls.

Black-and-white The first films were black-and-white, and their chemistry is still the basis of all films, even colour. Less complicated than colour negatives or slides, they have just one layer of emulsion, which simplifies the choice. Although manufacturers are always making improvements that may give one brand a temporary edge over others, you really need to choose only between slow, medium and fast black-and-white films.

Black-and-white film has a special place in photography – quite limited but important in several ways. Until just a generation ago, it was photography. As a result, many of the ideas, techniques and styles that defined photography were worked out in a monochrome palette of black, through grey, to white. Now that colour photography is almost universal, black-and-white has become very specialized. Few processing labs now handle it, so that most photographers working in black-and-white do the darkroom work themselves. But this is exactly part of the appeal of black-and-white photography – to be able to take a raw negative and manipulate the image. By means of custom processing and printing – in other words, doing it just to your specifications – you have an extra creative choice.

Even having made a print that you like, you can keep coming back to it to make different versions. The Italian reportage photographer Romano Cagnoni, with pictures spanning three decades, has said, 'I keep finding pictures that in the old days I ignored, and can find new ways of printing other negatives that emphasize different things.' Precisely because black-and-white photography works in a single range of tones, there is a range of films, processing chemicals and printing papers unavailable in colour. You can choose from these according to the effects you want.

There are important differences when you shoot in black-and-white. Shapes and tones become much more important, which gives you the chance to simplify an image, and reduce it to its essentials. If you are working in black-and-white for the first time, think of the colours in a scene only in terms of how bright they are, and make a special effort to ignore very strong colours – they may catch the eye, but will not translate into the photograph. One easy mistake is to be fooled by the obvious difference between two colours that in fact have similar tones – red and green, for example. In black-and-white, there will not be that difference, and those parts of the picture may merge.

Different black-and-white films Apart from normal silver-grain films of different speeds, there are a few specialized makes. Chromogenic film uses colour film chemistry to replace the silver grains with dye, and has great latitude, though not so permanent an image. Line or lith film records any image in just two tones, black and clear. It can be used for titles in a slide show or various special effects, such as sandwiching a silhouette with a second, background slide.

FILTERS FOR BLACK-AND-WHITE

Because black-and-white film records colours only as shades of grey, you can change them dramatically by using strongly coloured filters. A green leaf shot through a green filter will appear almost white; through a filter of its opposite colour, red, it will look virtually black. The same applies to other colours – use the same colour filter to lighten them, the opposite to darken. The effect only works well with strongly coloured subjects and a set of, perhaps, six filters of different strong colours gives you the means for exercising real control over the image. The table below lists the most common effects.

FILTER	COLOUR	EFFECT ON PICTURE	F. STOPS
8	Pale yellow	Makes blue sky appear natural. Reduces haze.	$+ \frac{2}{3}$
15	Deep yellow	Darkens blue sky. Reduces haze.	$+ 1\frac{1}{3}$
21	Orange	Darkens blue sky strongly and increases contrast outdoors. Darkens green vegetation. Lightens skin blemishes.	$+ 1$
25	Red	Darkens blue sky dramatically, increases contrast and deepens shadows outdoors (gives moonlit effect if slightly under-exposed.)	$+ 2\frac{1}{3}$
29	Dark red	Even more extreme than Wratten 25, darkening pale blue sky on horizon.	$+ 3\frac{1}{3}$
47	Blue	Exaggerates haze, increasing sense of depth in some landscapes. Turns blue sky white. Darkens yellows.	$+ 2\frac{2}{3}$
58	Green	Lightens greens, including vegetation. Darkens reds.	$+ 3$

Filters for colour films There are ranges of filters, some genuinely useful, many gimmicky, to alter the way light reaches the film. Most clip or screw onto the front of the lens, or fit into a special holder that attaches to the lens. The main types are described here, and they all have their uses. However, most of the time, in most photography, they are not strictly necessary.

Ultra-violet filters These are colourless or a pale yellow, and absorb the ultra-violet (UV) rays to which film is more sensitive than our eyes are. Without a UV filter, distant views have a blue cast and haze can soften the image, especially in mountains. This is particularly noticeable with telephoto lenses, as they magnify the distance. A practical benefit of using a UV filter is that it protects the lens from scratches and dirt.

Polarizing filters These filters darken blue skies and kill reflections in water and glass. They work by passing only light rays that are vibrating at a certain angle. Normally, light rays vibrate at all angles, but when they bounce off some surfaces they become polarized in one direction. A polarizing filter can block this light, and cut through haze for the same reason. Rotate the filter in its mount to vary the effect. It reduces exposure by about $1^{1}/_{3}$ stops. If you use one with a wide-angle lens, any blue sky will be unevenly darkened.

Graduated filters 'Grads', as they are commonly known, are half-tinted filters used mainly for darkening skies. Usually rectangular, the bottom half is clear, shading in the middle to a darker half above. Fitted in a special mount on the front of the lens, the filter can be moved up or down to coincide with the horizon line. This works more effectively with wide-angle lenses than telephotos, and you can make the transition zone more abrupt by stopping down the aperture. Neutral grads, available in different strengths (normally 1, 2 or 3 stops), are genuinely useful for balancing a cloudy sky with the landscape and for keeping rich colours in a sunset or sunrise without losing detail below. Coloured grads produce effects that usually look like gimmicks.

Light-balancing filters Either bluish or yellow-orange, and in different strengths, these are designed to correct the colour temperature of light (see pages 80-81) to white. In the Kodak series, the weakest filter for lowering colour temperature (81) is a pale straw colour, the strongest (85B) is orange. Their main uses are when photographing in the shade under an intense blue sky, or when using Type B films in daylight. The filters for raising colour temperature in the Kodak series range from 82 to 80A. Their main use is to make the light from tungsten lamps look less orange (see page 106).

Colour compensating filters In different strengths of the three primary light colours, red, green and blue, and their complementaries, cyan, magenta and yellow, these have mainly technical uses, such as when making duplicate slides. You can use them to make exact colour corrections, for instance to the

◀◀ *Balancing the image* The most obvious use for a graduated filter is to bring the brightness of the sky down to a level that is closer to the landscape. In this sunset scene (far left), the effect is to show the clouds in richer detail and colours, although the difference is only noticeable when seen side-by-side with an unfiltered shot (left).

▶ *Dual filters* Polarized light viewed through a polarizing filter can yield strange results. This plastic syringe (right) shows the multi-coloured effects of stress polarization. A large polarizing filter was placed behind it, and a polarizing filter over the lens. The filter was rotated for the maximum effect.

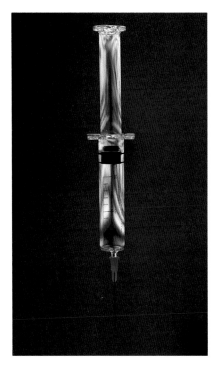

colour shift that happens with long exposures (see Reciprocity failure on pages 59-60). A magenta or red filter of about strength CC30 will correct most fluorescent strip-lighting (see below).

Fluorescent filters Strip-lighting of the kind found in offices and supermarkets looks white to the eye but usually appears greenish on film. These magenta/red filters compensate, although you cannot be certain how well, as the exact colour cast varies with the type of strip-light.

Neutral density filters In different strengths of grey, these simply reduce exposure. They have occasional technical uses, but hardly any in normal photography.

Effects filters This large category of filters produces various unusual effects, including softened edges, stars where there are points of light, prismatic colours, streaks of colour, and so on. Be careful in choosing to use this kind of filter. They may be fun to play with, and very occasionally indispensable in creating a particular image (such as a star or motion blur), but in normal photography they rarely appear anything other than contrived.

Colour as a subject To many people, colour simply occurs as part of a normal scene, and only stands out in any special way when there is a particularly vivid hue. This often translates into photographs in which the colour is secondary. The action in front of the camera may be far more important, or the graphic design. As most photography now is in colour, we tend to take the colour itself for granted, just as in the way we see.

Early photography was in black-and-white only, and some of the great photographic traditions grew up in this medium – reportage and landscape in particular. Though much less common now, black-and-white has kept a reputation for a kind of purity, and has had a certain artistic cachet.

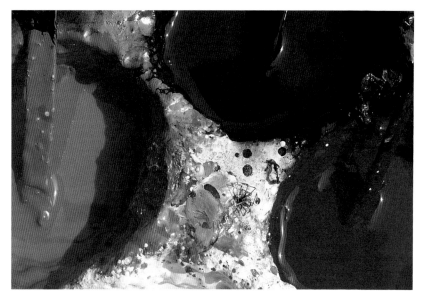

▲ *Pure hues* Colour itself – strong and sunlit – is the only subject in a close-up of a painter's palette (above). A macro lens was used to crop right in.

▶ *Unusual mixtures* This strange combination of grey and the orange reflection of a setting sun (right) was due to extreme summer haze.

By contrast, colour has often been considered less 'serious' than black-and-white, with few photographers treating it as a main element of image-making. Not everyone enjoys colours and the way they combine and react with each other, but if you do appreciate them visually, you can also make them a strong, distinctive part of your photographs. Look for the qualities of different colours, and the atmosphere that each helps to generate. Learn to distinguish between the different varieties of each colour, and look for scenes in which a colour is so important that you can treat it as the subject of the photograph.

Colour qualities Simply describing a colour as bright red, or lemon yellow, doesn't begin to do justice to the way it can work in a picture. If presented sympathetically, colours can be expressive – they can create or enhance atmosphere, working on a subjective level.

Just three qualities make a colour: hue, brilliance and saturation. Hue is what most of us mean when we say colour – red, or blue, orange, and so on. Brilliance is the level of brightness, and although some hues can be dark or light, others are limited – there are no really dark yellows, and no pale violets. Saturation is the purity – whether or not the hue is tainted with any other colour, which tends to muddy it.

▶ *Colour clarity* Yellow is the brightest of all pure colours. Setting it against a dark background, as in this food still life of a Japanese dish, enhances this essential quality.

The pure colours are those of the spectrum, which you can see in any well-defined rainbow. Although they merge from one to the next, it is usual to divide them into threes – three primary colours (red, yellow, blue) and three secondaries (green, purple, orange) which are their opposites. In nature, the most vivid colours occur less often than you might think, but when they do, they can put a powerful stamp on a photograph, as when one strong colour is used alone, or set against something neutral. Moreover, each hue has its own special qualities, both visual and expressive.

THE COLOUR CIRCLE

Pure colours form the spectrum, with primary and secondary colours blending via intermediary hues. The conventional way of showing them is arranged in a circle. This, the 12-hue colour circle, is the most usual. One advantage of showing them like this is that the colours facing each other across the circle are genuine opposites – or complementaries.

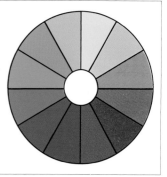

▲ **Expansiveness** *A clear sky is the most common source of blue (above). Clear atmosphere and a high altitude give the strongest blues, as in this landscape in New Mexico, exaggerated by a polarizing filter.*

◄ **Impact** *Red is arguably the most powerful and eye-catching colour – which is why it is used so much commercially, to command attention, as in this drive-in (left).*

◄ **Variation** *To the human eye, green is the most visible colour, but it comes in an extraordinary range of hues and tones. Some of the variety of green is hinted at in this shaded view of rain-forest on the Olympic Peninsula near Seattle (left).*

▲ ***Atmospheric colour*** *Haze softens light and colour, and combined with a low sun gives delicate pastels in this sunrise over the* *Camargue in southern France. Because it is more strongly filtered over distance, a telephoto lens enhances the effect.*

Softness and subtlety Pastels and what are called broken colours (mixed hues) are much more common than vivid hues, and in a photograph can usually stand a longer look. They can be subtle and interesting just because they are not so obvious. Part of their appeal is that the mixture of tints is not necessarily easy to recognize. The weather and lighting can soften colours. The atmosphere works rather like a filter; haze over a distance, or mist or fog all mute natural colours. Using a telephoto lens makes even more of this effect.

▲ *Seasonal colour The earthy tones of farmland in late summer give a characteristic range of soft colours where a poplar-lined road in Tuscany cuts through wheat fields.*

PALE AND UNSATURATED COLOURS

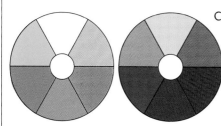

Pale   *Unsaturated*

Colours are less pure, and so softer, when they become lighter or less saturated. Lighter colours tend to look like pastel versions of the stronger hues, while un-saturated ones appear muddy and earthy. Here are the two corresponding versions of the basic colour circle.

Combining colours effectively Because colours are so charged with various qualities – visual and expressive – they have interesting effects when they are combined. There are many kinds of colour combination, as you can see in the pictures in this book and in real life. You can often select combinations by changing your viewpoint (to bring two colours closer together or cut one out), and by changing the lens to include more or less of the view.

COLOUR HARMONY

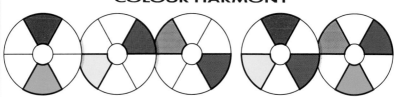

Colours that face each other exactly across the colour circle have a special relationship – they complement each other, which means they are mutually enhancing.Green is called the complementary of red, violet of yellow, and orange of blue. A balance of complementary colours can have great visual impact. There is also a three-way balance, such as between red, yellow and blue, and between green, violet and orange.

◀◀ *Natural harmony* In a hilltop cemetery at Lebanon Spring, New York (far left), warm light knits together the dark trees and pale stones.

◀ *Primary colours* A chance grouping of women going to market, seen on the island of Comoros off western Africa (left), brings together the classic three-way balance of the primary colours red, yellow and blue with vivid, fresh effect.

▶ *Complementary pairing* The red/green complementary contrast can be dazzling if both colours are bright, but at the Heian shrine in Kyoto (right) the vibrance of orange-red is balanced by a heavy, rich green.

Whether a particular combination of colours looks pleasant, jarring, interesting or uncomfortable depends partly on your personal taste, and partly on the actual colours. The centre of the colour circle is actually a mid-point of colour. Any colour mixed with the one opposite makes a neutral – white, grey or black. If you stare at one colour for a long time and then look away to a plain white surface, you will 'see' its opposite. All this means is that there is a special kind of balance of opposites. You can create harmony and balance in a picture using either related and similar colours, or by selecting the contrast of opposites.

In practice, the brightness of the different colours also needs to be taken into account. Red and green often have equal brightness and so 'balance' equally. Orange is lighter than blue, so the classic harmony is less orange and more blue. Yellow is much brighter than violet – they are opposites on the brightness scale of colours – and so works well when there is just a touch of it against a large area of violet.

Following this guide, however, by no means guarantees a good colour photograph, any more than slavishly dividing up the picture according to the Golden Section will make a good composition. There is no single ideal way of combining colours. Besides, you are at perfect liberty to follow your own preferences. Even if you choose an unconventional or strange colour arrangement, all that it means is that most people will not share your taste – and that doesn't necessarily matter.

Opposite qualities Similar colours form groups, and if you shoot within them you can bring a kind of unity to an image. The most obvious groupings are of cool or warm colours. These contrast with each other, not only across the colour circle, but also in the feeling they give to a picture. The colours on either side of orange, between yellow and red, seem physically warmer than their opposites on the colour circle, centred on blue-green. One group has all the connotations of heat, fire, dryness, the other suggests cold, ice, wetness. Visually, warm colours advance, cool colours recede (a reddish object always seems to stand out against a blue or green background).

▶ *Tints and shades If you are looking for a grouping that displays quite intensely the different aspects of one colour, a good solution is to move in close enough to eliminate any distracting or unharmonious elements. A girl picking roses near Yasenevo in Bulgaria (right) wears warm pinks and reds exactly suiting the occasion.*

▶▶ *Points of contrast Nature supplies a subtle harmony of cool blues and violets as dawn creeps into a Cornish harbour (far right). The uniformity of the palette is nicely enhanced by a brief element of contrast — where flashes of cold green and hot pink from the artificial lights are reflected in the water.*

Another way of identifying groups is whether the colours are light or dark. The darkest pure colour is violet, the lightest yellow. A photograph shot all in light colours will tend to look airy and cheerful, one in the dark end of the spectrum sombre and rich. Earth colours form a grouping of unsaturated hues. Browns, ochres, even brownish-purples, seem solid and natural, and have obvious associations with the earth.

A photographer has nothing like the choice that a painter has with colours, and there is no guarantee that you can manipulate them or shoot within a certain range. Your palette, however, is much bigger than in painting – it includes every ready-made colour in front of the camera, and you have some control in that you can select what to shoot.

METALLIC COLOURS

These have a special place in the scheme of colours. What makes them unique is that the play of light on them, and the way they reflect it, gives a very distinctive gradient of colour and tone. Metallic colours can add a dynamic touch to a photograph, but need care in lighting. If the surface is highly polished, a bright light source will create a hot spot, which can create extremes of contrast.

◄ *The selective eye* *Whereas you can set up a still life or interior shot to a chosen scheme of colour, outdoors you must deal with given components, but you can control the image by selection. Look for a strong balance of tones and a quality of light that paints the scene with special colour effects.*

The essential element As with colour, you can deal with light in a strictly practical way, or you can take a more sensual approach. The practicalities of light include making sure that enough of it reaches the film, that its direction suits the scene, and that its colour is more or less balanced. These are all essential, and are treated here, but they are also rather mechanical, and don't go far enough in handling one of photography's main ingredients.

The way the light falls on a face or on an object has a character that is not always easy to express in words. Occasionally, because of the weather, the angle of the sun, reflections or whatever, it creates a particular atmosphere that strikes a chord in someone looking at it. At moments like this, the light

can become the principal quality in the picture – and even the main subject. It is often easier to see this in certain paintings than in real life, but this is mainly a matter of training the eye.

Not every photograph needs this treatment – some subjects, as in reportage, are very strong in themselves – but if you learn to judge the light for its quality, it will lead you to images that you might otherwise not have noticed. It is easy to get carried away by the importance of lighting in a photograph, and it is only one of several elements that you have to juggle with in making an image. Nevertheless, it is almost entirely responsible for some important visual features in subjects and surfaces.

◄▲► *The unexpected pattern In all of these pictures, light has more than just a practical rôle. Because it is in some way slightly unusual, through the play of light and shade and the way it picks out certain parts of each scene, it can almost be regarded as the subject itself.*

For instance, light affects volume. However massive and deep an object may be, it will tend to look flat and weak in flat, shadowless lighting. Side-lighting, however, brings out the volume by throwing part of the subject into shadow. The softness or hardness of the light also affects its modelling properties – the slight softening on a hazy day, or from using an umbrella over a studio light, gives a smoother transition from light to shade and so rounder modelling.

Light can also show the shape of things more or less well. Cross-shadows confuse the shape, but a clear contrast between subject and background makes the most of it. Texture depends almost completely on lighting: usually what you see as texture is the pattern of tiny shadows on the surface.

Angle and intensity Raw natural lighting is a bright sun in a clear sky. Every other kind, from haze to cloud, is just a variation on this, in much the same way that you would adjust artificial lighting by diffusing it or reflecting it. Even if there is not a single cloud in the sky for the whole day, the quality of sunlight still changes. The biggest changes of all are early and late in the day, and these are dealt with on some of the following pages.

The direction of the sun makes a considerable difference, the more so when it is fairly low in the sky. There are two directions to think about – the sun in relation to the subject, and in relation to you. With a static subject like a building, the angle of the sunlight depends on the time of day, and on the season. To choose one direction over another, you need to plan the shot for a particular time.

Bright sunlight usually creates high contrast. The difference between the lit part of a subject and the shadows can often be more than colour slide film can handle. At times, this can be a problem, particularly if you are trying to give a clear view of something, but it can also add graphic interest to a picture. Because of the intensity of a bright sun, it casts reflections as well as shadows. The brighter the surface, the stronger they are. Off water or glass, for example, they can virtually be a second light source, while large light areas such as a white wall fill in shadows – useful if you are shooting a portrait on a bright day. Coloured surfaces can throw a cast into a picture that you may not notice at the time, such as a blue cast from a cloudless sky.

HINTS & TIPS

Where you see high contrast in stark sunlight, follow these guidelines:
- *Expose for the important details*
- *Compose to avoid heavy shadows*
- *Shoot at a different time of day*
- *Use fill-in flash*
- *Use lower contrast film*

◀ **Crispness and depth** *In clear air, early morning sunlight helps make shadows stand out sharply (left) and gives a feeling of depth to the view.*

▶ **Vivid colours** *Sunlight makes the most of strong, bright colours, like those of this Bulgarian festival costume (right).*

▲ **Close-up texture** *Like a spotlight that throws surface variations more dramatically into relief, angled sunlight is the ideal way of bringing out texture .*

Colour in light The colour of light changes during the day, particularly if the sky is clear. When the sun rises and sets, it can be orange or red, but during the middle of the day, when it is high, the light is what we think of as 'white', or normal. In the shade, if the sky is clear the light will be quite blue, although our eyes register this much less than does colour film. Similarly, at twilight the light can be blue, depending on the weather.

Normally, these colour differences in daylight hardly matter – and in fact add variety to photographs. Occasionally, however, it may be important for you to have normal, 'uncoloured' lighting – for instance, in a close portrait when you would usually want ordinary-looking skin tones. If so, the colour temperature of light is important – if you know the measurement, there are filters that you can use to correct or alter it.

Most light sources, like the sun or an electric lamp, work by burning. They are called incandescent lights, and their colour depends on how hot they are. From warm to very hot, the range of colours goes: red, orange, yellow, white and finally blue. The exact colour, whether of a setting sun or a table lamp,

| 10000 K | 9000 | 00 K | 7000 K | 6000 | |

▲ *Dusk*   ▲ *Midday*

Times of day *The orange-to-blue scale (top) shows the variations of colour temperature, related in the accompanying pictures to the light at different times of day. Strong sunlight at midday is white light, registering the colours most closely as we see them (above centre). Orange light such as appears at sunset (right) is lower in colour temperature, while blue falls much higher on the scale, as with twilight shades*

(above left). Film records these colours more sensitively, and therefore typically more intensely, than our eyes perceive them, because we adjust to the overall level of lighting in a given environment. Filters can help to control the colour values (see table, far right) but it is not always essential to use them: an intense red and orange cast in a sunset may be a desirable element of the image.

has a temperature, measured in Kelvins (K), which are similar to degrees Celsius but start at absolute zero. So, a candle burning orange has a colour temperature of around 2000 K, white light from a midday sun is about 5500 K, and open shade under a blue sky can be as much as 8000 or 9000 K. The light-balancing filters described on page 64 are designed to change these colours, and are shown in the table below. Most colour films are balanced for 'white' daylight at 5500 K, and need the filters listed in the first right-hand column, but a few films, called Type B, are balanced for 3200 K photographic tungsten lamps, and need the filters listed in the second right-hand column. For more on film types, see pages 58-59.

The reason why the colour temperature of daylight changes is because of the way that the atmosphere scatters it. When the sun is low on the horizon, its light passes through more atmosphere, and the molecules in the air scatter the shorter, bluer wavelengths more than the others. This makes the light redder. In the same way, if you look at a clear sky, you see these scattered blue wavelengths.

3000 K   2000 K

	DESCRIPTION OF CONDITIONS	FILTERS	
		Daylight	Type B
10000 K	Open shade under clear sky	85C	
9000 K			
8000 K			
7000 K	Overcast sky	81D 81B	
6000 K	Electronic flash Midday sun in summer		85B
5000 K		82A 82C 80D	85C
4000 K	2 hrs after sunrise & before sunset 1 hr after sunrise & before sunset 3200 K photographic tungsten lamp Sunrise and sunset	82A 82C 80D	85C
3000 K	100w tungsten lamp 40w tungsten lamp		82B 80D
2500 K			

▲ *Sunset*

Directional light The two extremes of lighting direction are when the sun is directly behind or in front of the camera. Side-lighting, with at least some shadows falling across the picture, is much more common. As with any situation in photography that is slightly unusual, front-lit and back-lit pictures can make a welcome difference, and even appear a little exotic. In one there are virtually no shadows and everything is illuminated; in the other the contrast is extreme and objects often appear in silhouette.

To make use of either of these lighting conditions, the sun must be fairly low – or else, in the case of front-lighting, you need to be on a high viewpoint looking down. Frontal lighting, with the sun directly behind you, gives its strongest effect if the sky is very clear. Under these conditions, and with colour film, the colours will be very intense and any bright or shiny surface will throw back strong reflections. If you photograph city buildings this way you can expect a strong glow from windows, particularly tinted ones. Because shadows are very thin or non-existent, there is some danger that the effect

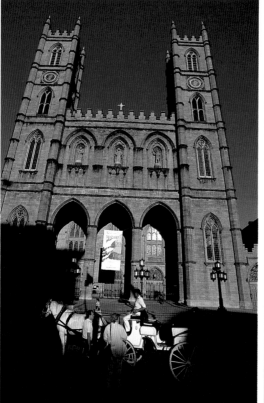

HINTS & TIPS

When shooting into the sun with a wide-angle lens, stop down the aperture as far as possible (select a slower shutter speed to suit) to give a star-like effect to the sun.

will simply look flat, which is why a clear sky is a big advantage for the intensity of the light. All of this is especially effective if you are lucky enough to have a sky ahead that is dark and stormy – then the contrast will be very powerful. One risk is catching your own shadow in the picture, particularly if you are close to the subject. If so, you may have to change your position slightly, or try to merge your shadow with that of something natural, like a nearby tree, rock or building.

Back-lighting is more varied in its effect, depending on whether you include the sun in the shot, hide it behind the subject, or have it just out of frame. The weather obviously makes a big difference – clouds can temporarily hide the sun, and even a slight haze can soften the contrast a great deal. Another variable is the lens you use. A telephoto will enlarge the sun and show it as a disc, while through a wide-angle lens it appears as a point of light. If you include the sun in the shot, never look at it directly unless it is on the horizon and very weak – you can damage your eyesight. Watch out for lens flare (see pages 92-93).

◀ *Front-lighting Provided that the air is clear, having the sun almost over your shoulder gives an intensity of light and colour that can produce very rich images. In the wide-angle view of the Basilica de Nôtre Dame in Montreal (far left), shadows from surrounding buildings heighten the contrast and pick out the calèche. In close-up, the wheel and side of a covered wagon (below left) look as sharp and bright as if photographed with an on-camera flash.*

▶ *Back-lighting This view of a man climbing a palm tree (right) relies not only on precise framing with a telephoto lens, but also on the single note of colour from the sun. The image of the sun was carefully positioned behind palm fronds so as not to overwhelm the scene.*

CLOUDS AND WEATHER

Interesting conditions A bright sun on a clear day may often seem like the perfect prescription for a photographic trip – the lighting is easy, pleasant and uncomplicated – but more often than not it is the weather and patterns of clouds that create interesting light and skies. The variety is infinite, from light, fair-weather cumulus clouds to a complete overcast.

The weather conditions change the lighting in a number of ways. Anything in front of the sun darkens it slightly, and on a stormy day there might not even be enough light to use fine-grained film in a normal way. More important, though, is what clouds do to the quality of light. Cloud cover softens shadows, and at the extreme of a really overcast day flatten the light completely; this kind of lighting is difficult to make look interesting, and the colour temperature will be a little higher than usual (an 81B or 81C filter can be useful). Ragged clouds give a patchwork of light and shade across a landscape, which can appear attractive from an overlook. Billowing white clouds can sometimes act as giant reflectors.

▲ *Varying effects Changes of weather have a profound effect on landscape, not just in the arrangement of light, shade and colour, but in the mood. These are identical views of Massachusetts marshes on the same day (above and top right).*

Rain Unless there is back-lighting or side-lighting from the sun, which is unlikely, it is difficult to catch falling rain on film. Usually, and at a distance, it looks like mist. To convey something of rain you need to include some of the obvious effects – ripples in a pond, drops on car roofs, umbrellas, and so on. On the rare occasions when the sun shines through rain, you can expect to see a rainbow. This is an optical effect, so if you move, it appears to move as well – you can use this to change the background. To capture the full arc of a rainbow, shoot with a wide-angle lens.

Fog It is often difficult to predict how long fog will last, and even a thick mist can sometimes clear in minutes. Make the most of it whenever you find it – the effects can be wonderfully atmospheric. Some of the most picturesque conditions are early in the morning when the fog is just light enough to show weak sunlight filtering through; shoot towards the sun for silhouettes of trees and other things in the foreground.

Lightning The unpredictability of lightning flashes is the main problem, but as long as you shoot at night or in the evening, you can leave the shutter open until one or more flashes make their own exposure on film. A wide-angle lens will increase your chances of getting them in the frame. The exposure is not critical, but as a rule, with ISO 50-100 film, use an aperture of about f4 for distant lightning over 10 miles (16 km), f5.6 for between about 2 and 10 miles (3 and 16 km). If the flashes are even nearer, f11 may be better, but then you probably should not be outdoors anyway.

▲ ▶ *Filling the frame*
Clouds make powerful subjects when weather conditions are dramatic. Adjust the framing to keep the horizon line low.

Changing light The hours around sunrise and sunset are special times for photography. If the sky is not overcast, the light is usually interesting, varied and very picturesque. There is a risk of cliché attached to these moments, as they have been photographed so many times and are used commercially in sugary ways, but this is precisely because so many people find them attractive. Every quality changes from minute to minute, and with the sun so low, you can often choose from front-, side- or back-lighting. A wide-angle lens will capture the full sweep of the sky, a telephoto can concentrate on the detail of colours, silhouettes and reflections.

▲ *A fresh view* The outline of the
Parthenon, Athens, is familiar enough to
work in silhouette (top) against a partly
cloudy sunrise from a nearby hill.

▲ *Capturing the mood* The remains of
storm clouds add to the spectacle of a
tropical sunset (above). Timing was important
to catch the right combination of elements.

◀ *Early light* Low-lying mist – more a
feature of sunrise than sunset – keeps
contrast low enough to shoot directly into the
sun in an Indian landscape (left).

Although the timing is important for the particular location, there is no
intrinsic difference between sunrise and sunset. In a photograph, if you were
not familiar with the place, you would find it impossible to tell the difference.
In the summer, sunset is usually a more convenient time to shoot – but there
are likely to be more people around. Sunrise often rewards early risers with
peaceful and empty scenery. Clouds can either kill or make a sunrise or
sunset view, and their effects are unpredictable. Stay on for dusk after the sun
has set, or at sunrise, try and set up the camera early enough to catch the
twilight (see pages 88-89).

Colour variations After the sun has set, and a little before it rises in the morning, the sky can go through some remarkable changes. This is twilight, when the sun lights the sky from below the horizon. How long it lasts, and what happens to the colours, depends on season and latitude. Summer twilight in northern parts of Europe and North America can last for a few hours; in the tropics less than an hour.

In a mainly clear sky, the colours shade from the horizon upwards, and can sometimes be intense. A classic twilight goes from orange on the horizon, through yellow, to deep blue. Occasionally, there is even a trace of green between the yellow and blue. High clouds sometimes light up briefly with a flash of red or orange after the sun has gone down.

To get the full range of this smooth gradation of colour and light, use a wide-angle lens, which takes in more of the sky. For detailed silhouettes of objects on the horizon, use a telephoto lens. In either case, bracket the exposure: more light on the film records more of the lit sky, but weaker colours, while a shorter exposure shows a narrower band of brightness with more intense hues. If the light level is too low for the camera's meter, switch to manual and change the film speed setting to the position for a faster film until you get a reading – then make allowance for the difference and remember to re-set the film speed. For example, if you are using ISO 50 film and get no reading, turn the setting to ISO 200 (four times faster). Whatever the reading shows, add two stops for the exposure.

▲ *Contrasting lights* An aerial
view of Miami just after sunset gave
just the right balance of lighting
between the sky and the street lights
(far left above). An earlier shot would
have been overwhelmed by the sun;
any later and the outline of the
coast would have disappeared.

▲ *Enhancing the image* Twilight
added colour and visual interest to a
viewpoint of the town of Sedona that
was otherwise only moderately
interesting (above).

◄ *Sky and land* Twilight provides
an evenly toned sky, which, reflected
in the water, gives the strongest
possible image of the river channels
in a mountain landscape (left).

Transformations Quite often, the whole character of a place changes throughout the day, as the sun moves through the sky. This happens slowly during the middle of the day (and, of course, at night) but at the changeover between day and night the light can change swiftly. A lot depends on the weather, and on whether the view is a natural landscape or a city. Although experience with sunrises and sunsets makes it easier to predict how the scene will change – and, importantly, which moment will look best – there are often surprises in the rapidity of the transformation. If the sky is overcast, little happens to the light – it just gets dimmer slowly.

◄ *Twenty-four hours* Four identical views of the City of London throughout a single day, passing from early morning (top left), through midday (bottom left), dusk (top right) and night-time (bottom right).

MOONLIGHT

Moonlight is actually sunlight — reflected. Too weak to measure with an ordinary meter, it is brightest when the moon is full and high in a clear sky. It is then about 400,000 times weaker than sunlight — around 19 f-stops — so work out the exposure from this. Also add extra time to allow for reciprocity failure (see page 59), and even more if the moon is less than full. As a starting point, try the following exposures — and bracket if possible. One problem with slow films is that adding more time to an already long exposure makes the reciprocity failure even worse.

Film speed	All at f 2.8
ISO 1600	30 sec
ISO 400	3 min
ISO 200	7 min
ISO 100	15 min
ISO 50	45 min

Photographing in moonlight Shooting a scene by moonlight requires very long exposures (see above), because the illumination is so weak. You can shorten the exposures slightly to achieve a darker, atmospheric night-time mood, but bracketing is advisable in any case.

If you are photographing the moon directly as a single subject, when it is full and clear in the night sky, shoot for 1/125 sec at f8 on ISO 50 or ISO 64. If the moon is crescent or its light is hazy, increase the exposure by a couple of stops or more. With a telephoto lens, use the fastest speed possible to avoid blur as the Earth turns.

Intrusive light Flare happens when light that is not part of the image reaches the film. Old-fashioned and cheap lenses are prone to it, but the real culprit is a bright source of light in front of the camera, most commonly when shooting towards the sun. The two hallmarks of flare are a line of bright polygons across the frame, caused by light striking the aperture diaphragm inside the lens, and an overall haze that weakens contrast and colour.

Flare also happens if your subject is surrounded by white – a close-up in the snow, for example, or a typical still-life 'product shot' on a white surface. You can make a quick check before shooting by lowering one hand in front of the lens; see if the picture in the viewfinder becomes crisper and slightly darker just before your hand comes into view. In fact, your hand, or a piece of card, makes an effective mask for flare, but the most convenient is a lens shade, of one of the types shown opposite.

Conventionally, flare is a problem to be avoided, and in most cases photographs look better when the lens is shaded. Nevertheless, you can make flare work to your advantage. With a telephoto lens, the overall flaring tends to spread light, and sometimes colour, all across the image. If there are pinpoint lights or reflections in the view, flare can sometimes give them a halo. Occasionally, the overlapping string of bright polygons can add to the feeling of the sun's intensity. As always, experiment for yourself.

▲▶ *Colouration Flare diffuses the orange glow of late afternoon sun through a telephoto lens (above) and enhances the sunlit mood of a 20mm landscape view (right).*

◀ *Special effects Flare from an aircraft window creates a fan of rays that, pointing downward into an aerial view of the Orinoco Delta, becomes an integral part of the composition (left).*

REDUCING THE RISK OF FLARE

• **Use a lens shade** Fit either a customized shade made by the camera manufacturer for your particular lens, or an independent make. The most efficient lens shade is one that masks right down to the edges of the picture frame, rectangular and adjustable, like a bellows shade. Many telephoto lenses have built-in shades that slide forward.

• **Keep the lens clean** A film of grease or dust makes flare much worse.

• **Remove any filter** Filters, however good, add another layer of glass that increases the risk of flare. Try removing any filters that might be fitted.

• **Use a properly coated lens** High quality multi-coated lenses give less flare than cheaper ones. Use the best optics you can possibly afford.

Simple black flag clamped in front of the lens

Screw-on or bayonet mounted shade

Adjustable bellows shade

GEOGRAPHICAL VARIATION

Mountain light In clear weather, this has a special intensity. The sky is a deeper blue, and shadows stronger, so that the contrast can sometimes be extreme. Because there is less atmosphere, there is much more ultra-violet than in the lowlands, and this can sometimes give unusual results on film if you are not prepared for it. Film is more sensitive than our eyes are to UV rays, and mountain views in sunny weather usually have a blue cast to the distance in photographs, particularly with telephoto lenses. There is not necessarily anything wrong with this – an advantage is that the blue haze gives a good impression of depth – but it does cut down on visibility. To overcome it, use a strong (that is, yellowish) UV filter and avoid shooting into the sun.

◄▼► *Atmospherics Clouds build and disperse quickly in mountainous landscape like the Himalayan foothills of northern Pakistan (left). Clear weather provides crisp visibility and intensely blue skies. The early morning shadows in an Andean village (right) have a typical blue cast. The view from the summit of Purace volcano in Colombia is stark in its contrasts and suffused with blue (below).*

▶ GEOGRAPHICAL VARIATION

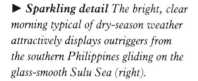

▲ *Sudden light* *The distant storm clouds common on tropical coastlines add to the drama of a Malaysian sunrise. The view is shown in the early half-light (top) and soon after the sun broke through (above).*

▶ *Sparkling detail* *The bright, clear morning typical of dry-season weather attractively displays outriggers from the southern Philippines gliding on the glass-smooth Sulu Sea (right).*

Mountains also have special weather patterns, that can change much more quickly than closer to sea level. Be prepared to take advantage of any change as soon as it happens, and do not rely on a slow progression of the light. At high altitudes, watch out for conditions when there are clouds below you – these can sometimes give you spectacular views of peaks standing like islands in a sea of cloud.

Tropical light In the tropics, the sun rises and sets at consistent times throughout the year. On the equator itself, daylight lasts exactly twelve hours every day of the year. Apart from being so predictable, the sun rises much higher in the sky than in mid-latitudes – by nine in the morning it is like a

midsummer noon elsewhere. For many subjects, particularly portraits of people, the light from a high sun is not very sympathetic: hard shadows are cast straight underneath. For some other subjects, like cityscapes, the starkness of tropical daylight can sometimes give a graphic edge to a photograph.

Polar light Near the poles, the sun never rises high, and in good weather this gives extended shooting time when the sun rakes the landscape. In midsummer, the sun's path is strange for anyone not used to it – going around rather than over the landscape. However, although summer conditions are specially good for photography, the winter offers little light, and for a very short time.

Sources and methods Outdoor artificial lighting comes in many forms, and is usually a mixture. Tungsten lamps are not now common, and most town and city lighting is a combination of sodium lamps (yellow, often as street lighting), vapour lamps (often bluish), and fluorescent lamps (usually greenish on film, although white to the eye). Individually and indoors, each of these types of lighting is a potential colour problem that calls for a filter, but mixed together in an outdoor scene the effect is simply colourful.

There are three basic ways of shooting in a city at night: hand-held with fast film, hand-held with regular film and flash, and a tripod with regular film.

HINTS & TIPS

Car headlights make useful emergency lighting if there is room to park in the right place. Use them to brighten up the foreground in a shot where there are lit buildings behind, or to pick out one particular subject. To soften the effect, tape tracing paper over the lamps.

For hand-held shooting, almost everything is sacrificed for a workable shutter speed: $^1/_{30}$ or $^1/_{60}$ sec is the minimum. Modern ultra-fast films, rated at around ISO 1600 make this possible. Use a fast lens if you have one, at full aperture, and bracket exposures – bright lights in view can throw some meters off. Flash photography at night is more limited in that you need to shoot from quite close and you cannot remain unobtrusive, but guarantees a sharp, clear view of fast movement. To show the setting and add atmosphere, try shooting with a shutter speed slow enough to record the lights, even if blurred. With a tripod, you can treat night-time cityscapes very differently. With a time-exposure, this is the ideal technique for static shots, but any movement in an exposure of (typically) a few seconds, will translate into a blur. However, views that include traffic can work very successfully – the headlights and tail-lights become streaks of colour that pick out the streets.

FIREWORKS

These only work properly on film in a time exposure – the trails of light from a burst create the shapes and colours. In effect, let the fireworks display make its own exposure by using a tripod and opening the shutter for several seconds. Use an aperture of around f2.8 with ISO 50 or ISO 100 film, set the shutter to T or B, and time the exposure to coincide with a burst.

▲ **Reflected light** A faint mist over the City of London reflects some of the street lighting, and holds the outline of the buildings in a telephoto shot (top).

▲ **Light in motion** A time exposure at a temple festival turns lanterns in a procession into streams of light (above).

▶ **Floodlighting** The waterfront of the old port and the floodlit Nôtre-Dame-de-la-Garde, Marseilles (right).

Light sources and colours Artificial lighting that is not designed specifically for photography, called available light, is usually tungsten, fluorescent or vapour lighting, and the way its colour appears on film is usually the main concern. Ultra-fast films have opened up this area of photography – scenes that before could only be treated in a rather rudimentary way with flash can now be photographed normally. The only price to pay is graininess.

First, find out exactly what type of lighting is installed. Fluorescent strip lamps, which are probably the most common of all, behave strangely with colour film. Typically, they appear neutral white, but in fact they don't emit a full spectrum. The result is that most give a greenish cast to colour film. The exact colour varies, but can normally be taken care of with a proprietary fluorescent filter coloured between magenta and red (see below). Two rare exceptions are colour-corrected strip-lights that do look white on film, and a kind that records reddish.

Tungsten lighting in domestic interiors is fairly predictable, and falls on the colour temperature scale (see table on page 81). How orange it appears depends on the wattage. Vapour lamps are common in factories and similar large interiors. Sodium vapour is yellow, and no amount of filtration will neutralize it. Mercury vapour is bluish, but multi-vapour (used in sports stadiums for televising of night events) is colour-corrected. Before worrying about filtration, however, consider whether it is worth trying to correct the colour. Quite often a slight cast does not matter.

CORRECTING ARTIFICIAL LIGHTS

The eye gets used to tungsten lighting and usually sees it as less orange than it really is. Fluorescent lighting looks white, but records green, while sodium vapour lamps are uncorrectable – they emit only a narrow band of the spectrum, so adding blue just makes them appear a darker, greener yellow. Mercury vapour and multi-vapour lamps often look the same to the eye, but the latter are corrected.

	DESCRIPTION	CORRECT WITH
TUNGSTEN	Deep to pale orange	Bluish
FLUORESCENT	Blue-green to green	Red/magenta
SODIUM VAPOUR	Yellow-green to yellow	Not possible
MERCURY VAPOUR	Blue-green to pale blue	Red
MULTI-VAPOUR	Pale blue to white	Straw or nothing

◀ *Uncorrected colour* Tungsten lighting bathes a Japanese market for tuna fish before dawn. ISO 200 Kodachrome was fast enough with an f1.8 lens. The orange cast is perfectly acceptable, and not fitting a blue filter saved valuable exposure (left).

◀ *Eliminating colour cast* The principal lighting in London's Stock Exchange is fluorescent (left), which a standard FL filter corrected perfectly.

▼ *Arresting colour* The lighting in this jade vault is greenish fluorescent (below), but the tungsten lamp being used for inspection offsets it visually. The shot was taken unfiltered.

On-camera flash Now virtually perfected, flash is the exclusive lighting for still photography. Its advantage is that it is fast and predictable and, if mounted on the camera, very easy to use. Against this, it completely changes the 'real' lighting of a room or a subject, and usually has no pretence to naturalness. Also, as you can't preview the effect (except by taking a Polaroid test), there is some uncertainty as to how the picture will look.

Although a few types of flash bulb are still available, flash is almost exclusively electronic. Most common is on-camera portable flash, sometimes built in. In a modern automated camera, the flash can be integrated into the system so that not only is the flash exposure metered, but made to balance with the normal lighting. If the subject is in shadow against a brightly lit background, for example, it is normal for the flash output to be controlled so that it just fills in the darker areas. Other sophistications are zoom flash, in which the angle of the flash output changes automatically when you alter the focal length of a zoom lens, and rear-curtain flash, in which the flash is triggered at the end of an exposure. Rear-curtain flash is useful in a slow exposure recording available light: if you photograph someone walking, the blurring of the movement by available light leads up to the sharp flash-lit image.

▶ *Double lighting*
Using a second flash in sync gives the option of lighting the background separately. In this case, the background flash was filtered and aimed at a white sheet of paper.

The real limitation of on-camera flash is that its direction and light quality are both about the least flattering. For the extra effort of planning and setting up lights, you can achieve a much wider range of effects with more powerful, separately triggered flash heads. There are two kinds: high-output portable flash powered by rechargeable batteries, and mains-powered flash, which is normally used in studios. Both can be used with a variety of fittings, and it is these – the diffusers, reflectors and spots – controlling the quality of the light that make all the difference. You should take as much care of this lighting quality as you would in choosing natural light.

FLASH EXPOSURE

Nearly all on-camera flash units are in some way integrated into the camera's metering system. If not, they have their own automatic sensors which, even in the most basic units, are straightforward to operate. Non-reflex cameras have leaf shutters in the lens, and these can synchronize with the flash at any speed. Single lens reflex cameras, however, have a problem with synchronization at high shutter speeds (when the size of the gap between the two shutter curtains narrows). This is due to the time it takes for the energy of the flash to be discharged, as compared to the speed at which the shutter moves. The highest shutter speed that can be used with the flash is marked on the shutter speed dial. For off-camera flash, such as you would be using in a studio, a hand-held flash meter is essential.

▶ *Close-up accuracy Studio flash is irreplaceable for photographs that include people and movement – and in particular, where the skin tones must be accurate. For this shot of a model wearing a pearl necklace, a 1000-joule flash was fitted with a soft-box diffuser to reduce harsh shadows.*

HINTS & TIPS

Ring flash is a special design of on-camera flash in which the tube is circular and surrounds the front of the lens. The effect is completely shadowless lighting. You may find this useful in close-up photography, when there is not room for an ordinary light between the lens and the subject; but make use of its unusual effect occasionally, not as a rule.

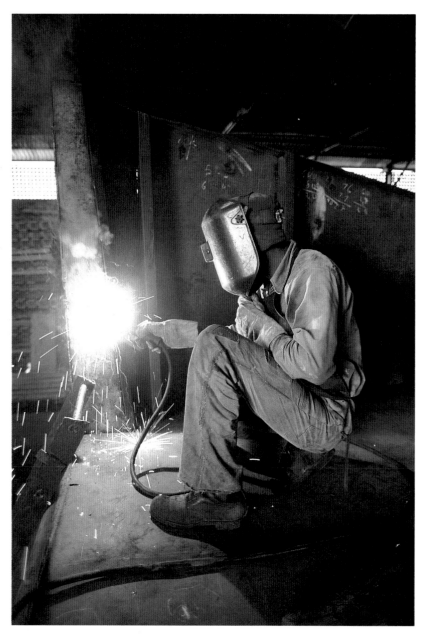

▲ **Enhancing detail** Among the most useful jobs that an on-camera flash can perform is the basic, if unexciting one of filling in foreground details, as in this photograph of a welder, where the foreground area would otherwise be dark.

FLASH EQUIPMENT

◀ *Free-standing mains-powered unit*

▼ *Studio lights Small mains-powered units (below left) have output of between 200 and 800 joules. Area lights (below) give diffused but directional lighting.*

▲ *Umbrellas Depending on the material it is made from, an umbrella attachment diffuses the light of the flash or reflects it back onto the subject. Translucent fabric (above left) gives soft diffusion, while the opaque white umbrella (above centre) creates a harder light. The aluminium umbrella (above right) gives a very hard quality.*

▶ *Screens A diffusing screen, made from any of various suitable types of translucent material, can be propped up or hung in the required position.*

Consistency and continuity Although it may seem a little old-fashioned compared with flash, photographic tungsten lighting has the virtues of being very simple, easy to use, and continuous. Because it is continuous, there are no technical problems about synchronization or doubts about how the image will look – what you see is what you get. The colour, of course, is more orange than daylight; but if you are using only these lights in a darkened room or studio, Type B film is balanced for it. If you want to mix tungsten with daylight (or any other lights, for that matter), it is a simple matter to fit the appropriate filter over the light head.

Because the effect of a tungsten light can be judged on the spot, many heads have some means of adjusting the spread of the beam, such as by moving the lamp in and out of the reflector bowl, angling reflector panels, or moving a lens inside the housing. In addition, barn doors (flaps attached to the front of the light) are used to mask down the area covered. The advantages and disadvantages of tungsten and flash are listed below, but in practice they tend to be used for different kinds of subject.

	ADVANTAGES	DISADVANTAGES
TUNGSTEN	■ Photographs the way it looks ■ Good for large, static subject – just increase the exposure time ■ Mechancally simple, little to go wrong ■ Easy to use ■ Can use to show streaked movement ■ Some units very small and portable	■ Not bright enough to freeze fast movement ■ Hot, so can't accept some diffusing fittings, and dangerous for some subjects ■ Needs blue filters to mix with daylight
FLASHLIGHT	■ Stops any fast action ■ Cool, quick to use ■ Daylight-balanced, mixes easily	■ No pre-view with small units, others need modelling lamps used in relative darkness ■ Fixed upper limit to exposure, beyond which needs multiple flash ■ Technically complex

There are various types of light filters used with tungsten lighting. The following is a guideline on the filters most commonly applied to balancing tungsten with a daylight source (for information on colour temperature, see also pages 80-81). A full blue filter adjusts the colour temperature, converting 3200 K tungsten to 5500 K daylight; a half-blue filter makes a partial correction and boots the colour temperature of a domestic lamp. An 85 filter converts 5500 K daylight from a window to match the quality of tungsten lamps within the room; half-CTO provides partial correction.

TUNGSTEN LIGHTING EQUIPMENT

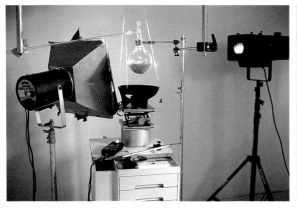

▲ **Continuous lighting** To photograph a flask of rose petals being distilled for perfume, an arrangement of tungsten lamps was ideal for illuminating the detail in a static but reflective subject (above).

◀ **Light sources** The large bulb (centre left) is a standard 275-watt photographic lamp with screw fitting. The smaller tungsten-halogen lamps, at 250-watt (far left) and 650, 1000 or 1250-watt (left), are more efficient, as the tungsten filament burns at higher temperature in halogen.

▶ **Light housings** All types of housings include a reflector behind the lamp that throws back radiating light to maximize the illumination. Movable flaps may also act as reflectors, or as 'barn doors' that concentrate or restrict the beam (right).

SUBJECTS AND THEMES

Character and expression The ingredients of a good, basic portrait photograph are simple enough: a sympathetic view that captures not just the physical likeness but something of the person's character – at least as the photographer or the subject sees it. Simplicity, in fact, is something of a catchword when photographing people. The human face is interesting enough without complicated technique or unusual composition, and if you can catch the right expression, that alone will usually make the picture successful.

▶ *Relaxing the subject A 'prop' is always useful if there is an obvious one to hand; in this case the unusual choice is another live model – the lamb. Holding it gave the girl no opportunity to feel self-conscious (right).*

▶▶ *Capturing the mood For an animated expression in an impromptu portrait, the moment is everything. The candid smile on the faces of these two men in an Athens workshop (far right) was obviously fleeting, and had to be shot without any hesitation.*

One of the keys to achieving this artless simplicity is being able to encourage people to relax and act normally – not to restrict themselves in a stiff pose, but not to put on an act, either. Photographic technique apart, the most valuable skill you can acquire is to be outgoing, and to put people at their ease and help them lose their self-consciousness.

A portrait does not have to be shot in a studio, and does not even have to be planned. Many of the best are impromptu – taken on the spur of the moment because the photographer seized the opportunity in the right situation. Indeed, one absolutely essential technique (there are very few in any case) is to shoot immediately you see that the expression or gesture of your subject is right – without any hesitation at all. This applies to both candid shots and posed pictures. Delays and fumbling account for more lost good portraits than anything else – it takes very little time for a spontaneous grin to fuse into a grimace.

In terms of the photographic technique – setting, lighting and composition – this means that you must work quickly, even if there isn't really enough time to prepare things perfectly. The simpler the setting, as a rule, the better – a plain, unobtrusive background, or at least one that doesn't fight for attention with the subject. The occasion is also a part of this – you are less likely to be successful coaxing somebody out of a bad mood than choosing a time when a group of friends are enjoying themselves.

There are no actual rules for lighting, but in the interests of simplicity, soft, hazy sunlight is probably the easiest to deal with, while hard sunshine is usually the worst (it creates strong shadows, and encourages a tendency for people to screw their eyes up and squint). On the whole, diffuse light serves a quick, uncomplicated portrait well. A reflector on the shadowed side of the face can help – either a purpose-made collapsible one or an available one within the setting, like a white wall.

Composing a portrait is mainly a matter of deciding how closely to frame the shot on the face. The four obvious options for basic composition are a head shot, head-and-shoulders, three-quarter shot (head and torso), and a full-figure shot that inevitably shows something of the setting. Only the last really suits a normal or wide-angle lens. The most flattering perspective for the face is obtained with a telephoto lens – the most popular choices for portraits are between about 85mm and 150mm.

▶ **PORTRAITS**

▲ *Informality This painter felt uncomfortable looking straight to camera, and the obvious solution was for him to occupy himself working (above).*

◀ *Context A French chef in the natural setting of her restaurant (left) made for an uncomplicated but effective portrait, lit by tungsten lamps to match the ambient lighting.*

Lighting a portrait Professional photographers often need to set up portrait sessions well in advance, particularly if the photograph is to be taken indoors with lighting. This makes it possible to be inventive and to guarantee a particular type of image. Technically, there are three basic choices for lighting:

• Use natural daylight, with shadow fill as necessary from a flash, other light or reflector.
• Use available room lighting, perhaps adding a little photographic lighting.
• Use only photographic lights (either flash or tungsten).

SIX WAYS TO IMPROVE A PORTRAIT

1 Lens: Use a telephoto for more flattering proportions. With a 35mm camera, select a focal length long enough to flatter the face, but not so long that it needs to be used from a great distance.

2 Depth: Set the aperture to no smaller than two stops down (for example, with an f 2.8 lens, shoot at f 4 or f 5.6). Focus on the eyes, and the background will be pleasantly soft, making the person stand out clearly.

3 Light: Diffuse the main light and place it slightly in front of the subject, somewhere between nearly overhead and to the side. With a photographic light, an umbrella is the easiest diffuser to use, but soft daylight from a window also works well. In any case, place the subject close to the light and use a reflector on the shadow side of the face.

Full-figure poses
There are many
informal variations
you can try.

4 Pose: There are no hard and fast rules, but if you ask your subject to lean forward slightly towards the camera, they will usually look more interesting and alert. A fail-safe pose is to sit the person down with a surface to lean on, like a table, shoot from a slight angle to the body with the head turned towards the camera.

5 Atmosphere: Try to relax your subject — it helps if you look as if you know what you're doing. Keeping up a flow of conversation nearly always works, and animates the expression. Beware, however, of catching the subject with his or her mouth open. If the expression starts to freeze, ask the subject to look away for a moment, and then back at the camera.

6 Film: Shoot lots of it. More than anything else, this helps to relax a nervous sitter, who doesn't feel the need so much to hold an expression.

Whichever you choose, you will probably find that softer rather than harder lighting suits most faces. One of the most basic and reliable lighting set-ups features one main light, diffused (such as with an umbrella), positioned a little above the face, to one side and in front. A weaker second light or silvered reflector fills in shadows (crumpled cooking foil can be used if you have to improvise); a spotlight from a distance behind can highlight hair or the side of the face. There are, of course, as many ways of lighting a face as there are portrait photographers, and it is worth taking time to experiment with different styles.

The story-telling image One of the classic uses of the camera is reportage photography. Essentially, this covers all the ways in which people behave and interact with each other. Reportage is different from news photography in that it tries to look a little deeper into the human condition, though the two sometimes overlap. Many of the best reportage photographs have a timeless element to them. The human face, and the gestures of the body, can be very expressive indeed – not only about the immediate circumstances, but about life in general.

▲ *Instant reaction A moment of hilarity glimpsed down an alleyway in Athens (above), photographed with a 400mm lens, hand-held.*

◀ *Association An obvious juxtaposition – of the kind intended by the sculptor who installed this bronze of a seated figure in a shopping mall (left).*

Reportage photography has a strong story-telling element, if you treat this broadly. The 'story' may be an unusual activity or an everyday event, or an emotion or reaction. It may be an association between people or between people and things that only you can see in the viewfinder. You find it in a single shot, or in a set of pictures. What counts very strongly is that the images are well timed – that you catch an expressions and gestures that are alive. For pictures of people behaving naturally – not posing for the camera – it is virtually essential to shoot without being noticed.

◀ *Representing an event A player in a small brass band gives the flavour of the occasion. People performing, even on a small scale like this, are generally easy, uncomplicated subjects to photograph.*

◀ *Describing a locality Café life is another readily available source of reportage subjects. Sidewalk cafés in particular offer a constantly changing parade of people, usually in good lighting.*

◀ *Private and public The camera catches an intimate moment between a couple in a park. Even with a medium telephoto lens as used here, there is usually only time for one or two shots without being noticed.*

The art of observation There are a few ways of photographing people unobserved, and not all of them involve being hidden. The most direct way is simply to shoot very quickly, quietly and without fuss. This is easily enough said, and some great reportage photographers like Henri Cartier-Bresson have made this approach their hallmark, but it needs astute observation and fast reactions.

Observing people, even without a camera, is an art in itself, but something you can practice all the time. Try to anticipate what people will do next in any kind of situation – how they will react or look – because this will give you an edge in the next step of catching the expression or movement on film. When you see the moment that you think is right, shoot without hesitating. Most people pause out of uncertainty before pressing the shutter, but the more you use your camera, the faster you should become. Small, quiet cameras are ideal, and auto-focus simplifies quick-reaction shots, provided that the system works virtually instantly.

For this kind of photography, particularly in the street or other public place, like a market, a standard or wide-angle lens is probably best. Either type allows you to shoot from fairly close, which is useful if there are a lot of people around who might otherwise get in the way of a shot. The difficulty is that people can also see you, which may make it impossible to get a second natural-looking shot. A wide-angle lens of, say 24mm, can help in this. If you compose the view so that the person you want to photograph is off-centre, it will appear as if you are aiming the camera to one side.

HINTS & TIPS

If you really don't want to look like a photographer but still need to carry a reasonable amount of equipment, buy a cheap small bag with a strap for carrying the cameras and lenses. The more ordinary and unremarkable it is, the less noticeable you will be.

▶ *Active contrast The trompe l'oeil painting on a street corner made an appealing subject – but was clearly stronger with someone passing. The shot was timed for the woman to be just clear of the painting.*

▲ *Incorporating a reaction* A quick unobserved market shot (above) turned into more of a portrait when the shopper spotted the photographer.

▼ *Expressive detail* Stay alert for interesting expressions (below) – easiest to catch with a wide-angle lens which is unlikely to need re-focusing.

▲ *Stillness* Two men idling the afternoon away on the sidewalk of an Andean town remain quite unaware of the photographer's presence. The picture, obtained with a 180mm lens from across the street, has the timeless mood often typical of reportage.

Keeping your distance You can make good use of longer lenses, though in a different way from a wide-angle lens. A telephoto lets you stand at a distance from the people you are photographing, and there is every chance that you will not be noticed. A medium telephoto – say, 180mm – is particularly good for 'across-the-street' shots for framing a full-length figure, and for full-face shots from a few metres. Longer telephotos, such as 300mm and 400mm, are trickier to use – they are heavier, need a faster shutter speed to overcome camera shake, but have smaller maximum apertures. One of the best ways of using them is from somewhere that you can sit quietly for a while without drawing attention, such as a sidewalk cafe. With all telephotos, watch out for other people, or cars, crossing in front of the camera and spoiling a shot.

If you are using a wide-angle lens, with practice you will gain a fairly good idea of what the lens will take in without looking through the viewfinder. If so, you can shoot very discreetly with an auto-focus camera – hold it lower than usual, and look away as you squeeze the shutter release.

▲ *Movement The regular actions of children diving into a fountain (above left) allowed time to wait for just the right moment.*

▲ *Gesture A momentary gesture perfectly completes the shot of bathers in a thermal sulphur spring in Tuscany (above right).*

THE PICTURE ESSAY

Because there is a story-telling component to reportage photography, it lends itself particularly well to a set of pictures covering a common theme. In professional magazine photography this is the picture essay, which tells the story through a number of juxtaposed photographs, not necessarily in sequence. It is important to have variety in the final set of images.

Defining a context One of the most rewarding, and straightforward, situations for photographing people naturally is when they are engaged in their normal working activity. Not only is it what most people do for most of each day, it is not usually considered private. Far from intruding, a photographer is often welcome. When people take a pride in their work, they are naturally flattered by the attention of someone who is seriously interested in what they are doing. The exceptions are when the photographer gets in the way of a job and interferes with it or slows it down, or if the person you are photographing actually considers the work demeaning – the latter can be a problem in urban ghettoes and some poorer countries. Usually, however, if you make a reasonable approach you will get a sympathetic, if sometimes puzzled, reaction.

What can make this subject rewarding to photograph is that work provides the occasion for people to exert themselves, physically and mentally. Some jobs are more interesting visually than others, but all have their particular rhythms and complexities.

▲ *Descriptive images* Your approach to photographic composition can emphasize the character of the work, as in these studies of Bulgarian students gathering the annual rose harvest (top) and man and machine quarrying marble at Carrara (above).

▲ *Dramatic impact* Loading freight into a ship in the harbour of Piraeus, near Athens. The semi-abstract silhouette was achieved by waiting for the load to block out the sun, and under-exposing the shot (above).

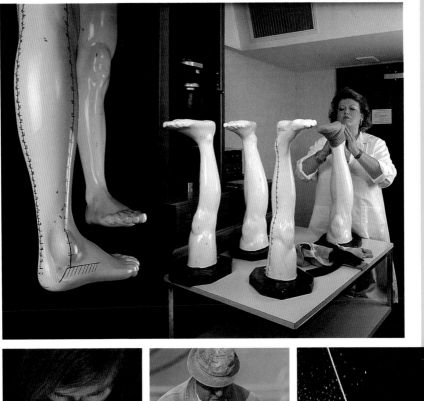

▲ *Exploring detail* Even mundane jobs can be visually interesting, but look for unusual or attractive detail and make sure you choose a suitable scale that includes the important features of the image. These pictures show a quality-check on socks for a major retail store (top); carving the wax master for a watermark used in security printing (above left); writing out dockside prices for the morning's catch of fish (centre); scaling the hull of a ship in dry dock (above right).

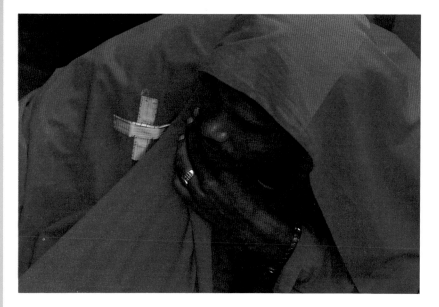

Working in crowds Parades, fairs and other public showcase events offer some of the richest and most colourful possibilities for photography. The only usual difficulty is working your way around the crowds. Finding the right viewpoint for the right moment is essential, and the key to this is planning. Most events are organized, at least to some extent, and you can usually expect to find viewpoints and work out the timing in advance.

If you have enough time in the days before the event, get a schedule from the organizers or the local newspaper, then look around the site or route to find the best vantage points. If the event is very popular and likely to be

Capturing the whole event
A variety of images from a
festival held on Corpus
Christi day in a Venezuelan
town. It centres on a dance of
devils, wearing locally made
papier maché masks and red
costumes. Rehearsals (right),
the dance itself (far left),
spectators (left) and moments
of rest (bottom left) each
provide different subjects for
the camera.

covered by the media, the very best positions are likely to be reserved, but even then doing your own groundwork can turn up a free viewpoint. Also, there is no harm in asking if you can enter the area set aside for the press – there is always a chance if the occasion is relaxed.

HINTS & TIPS

The best view of a parade is often seen head-on with a telephoto lens. A bend in the road or a traffic island are likely to be good positions for this, unless restricted. Some professional photographers who are used to covering special events carry a short, lightweight step-ladder to guarantee a clear view over crowds.

Somewhere high, like a balcony or the roof of a building, is often a good, safe bet, allowing you a variety of images with different lenses. Even a slightly elevated position is useful for shooting over the heads of crowds – if you are checking before the day, anticipate where other people will be. The disadvantage is likely to be that, once in place on the day, everywhere may be so crowded that you can't move. If you know that you will have to stay in one fixed position, take more rather than less equipment – a tripod, for instance, is useful with long lenses (just loosen the head when you use it so that you can pan around the scene). On the other hand, if you are going to be on the move, take only what will fit easily into one bag.

Take more film than you think you will need – these occasions encourage heavy shooting – and if possible carry two loaded camera bodies so that there is no risk of losing a shot at a key moment. Most events, in fact, turn around one or two key moments, such as the high point of a procession. Try to make sure you get these, but don't ignore all the other possibilities. These include the unpredictable events, behind-the-scenes preparations, and the faces and reactions of spectators.

▶ **BUILDINGS**

▶ *Exploiting texture Close in on architectural detail and the specific qualities of building materials to create or enhance the visual interest of your picture. The examples here show nineteenth-century ornament on the façade of a hotel in Fremantle, Australia (right) and an Icelandic house made of corrugated iron (far right).*

Sympathetic treatment At its best, architecture is art, and deserves some care and interpretation in photography. If you are taking a picture of a building of any consequence, first take some time to study its design and function. For instance, what was the architect's intention? Was it designed to be imposing, or to make the best use of available space, to make a particular visual statement, or to blend in with the surroundings? Was it designed for a single best view? Does it have one feature that is remarkable, or at least more important than any other? These are the kinds of questions that should guide you towards a particular treatment and viewpoint.

As with most static subjects in photography, viewpoint is always an issue, and sometimes the most important ingredient in the image. Study all the options by walking around the building and viewing from different distances. Sometimes a telephoto view from a distance will give a 'closer' view than a wide-angle shot from just in front. A frame-filling picture of the façade has impact, but you may prefer a view that shows the building in its wider setting, or a tightly cropped view of a representative part.

Although you may not be able to rely on the light, work out in advance what the ideal daylight conditions would be – in particular, the angle of the sun. If you are shooting in black-and-white, a yellow, orange or red filter to darken the sky can help to dramatize a shot.

▲ *Variations on a theme Two lighting treatments of the Jefferson Memorial in* *Washington DC, both at sunrise, from opposite sides of the building.*

CONVERGING VERTICALS

To see lines converging on the horizon is a normal effect of perspective, an optical illusion that helps to describe space and distance. There is a similar effect with vertical lines that continue far above eye level – the sides of a tall building, for example – but the eye is less accustomed to converging verticals and does not so readily accept them as normal in a photograph. You can choose to make them an exaggerated and obviously intentional feature by using a very wide-angle lens, but generally they are best avoided.

The practical problem is that to take in all of a building from a close viewpoint, you would usually need to tilt the camera upwards, thereby emphasizing the distortion. The ways of overcoming this mostly rely on keeping a horizontal aim:

• The ideal is a perspective-correction (PC) or shift lens, which works by covering an area larger than the film frame. Working a rack-and-pinion slides the front part of the lens upwards, bringing the upper part of the image down into the frame. So, you can aim the camera horizontally and still include the top.

• Look for a higher viewpoint, such as half-way up the building opposite.

• Use a wide-angle lens, aim the camera horizontally so that the building's sides stay vertical, and move far enough away to include everything. Crop off the lower foreground when making the print.

• Use a wide-angle lens in the same way as above, but compose the shot to include some relevant foreground interest, such as a flower bed or an ornamental pond.

• Move much further back and use a telephoto lens.

◄ ► *Perspective correction*
Avoid converging verticals by
setting the building back and
using the foreground, as in this
view of the US Supreme Court
(far right). A 28mm shift lens
was used for the façade of an
Italian church (left), creating
typical stretch distortion close to
the top of the frame. By
contrast, aggressively modern
buildings may be suited to a
strongly angled view (right).

▲ CITYSCAPES

Taking a view You can treat cities and towns in much the same way as landscapes, and not just as a location for photographing people. Of course, human activity or its signs are always present, so that cityscapes inevitably show something of the relationship between people and environment.

Viewpoint is usually the first thing to consider, and tends to be more of a problem than in a natural landscape. You don't have unrestricted access from different angles, and the layout of buildings always narrows the choices of clear views. Cities surrounded by or built on hills have many good viewpoints, but they are the exception. Some of the most effective shots are those taken at a distance and at height with a telephoto lens.

HINTS & TIPS

For a night-time shot, cities are more brightly lit after sunset than before sunrise, and more so in winter than summer. Different types of light – street lighting, neon displays and public building spotlights – are switched on at different times. You may have to check the scene the evening before to guarantee the timing for the brightest array of lights.

◄◄ *Scale and detail*
Ornate wrought-iron balconies
are characteristic of New
Orleans' French Quarter (far
left). The figure of a man
adds a focus of interest.

◄ *City moods* A *San*
Francisco street (left) is
photographed partly as a
reflection in a shop window
for a sense of the jumble and
activity of a downtown
city area.

When you are looking for a vantage point that enables you to show the spread of your subject, try the following:

● The top of any prominent tall building. High-rise residential blocks sometimes have open access, some public buildings may have purpose-built viewing galleries, but for offices and official buildings you would normally need advance permission.
● Any high ground, such as a hillside.
● The opposite side of a stretch of open ground or water, such as in a park, or on the furthest bank of a river.

Anticipate the lighting conditions that will give the effect you want. As with landscapes, a low sun in the early morning or late afternoon is usually more attractive than a high sun. Midday sunlight usually gives more contrast in a city than in an open landscape, as tall buildings cast large, strong shadows. (In daylight, you may wish to move in closer to pick up architectural detail.) Sunrise and sunset can be as effective in urban locations as anywhere else. Cities also usually look good after dark, especially at dusk when there is still enough light to show the shapes of buildings.

MONUMENTS

Atmospheric locations Archaeological sites call for many of the same camera techniques as regular buildings, but there are some other things to consider. Some of the more remote, or extensive, sites offer possibilities for very evocative photography. The temples of Angkor in Cambodia, shown here, are perfect examples of this kind of monument: too large and overgrown to be dominated by visitors, they give plenty of opportunities for exploring with the camera. On a smaller scale, there are similarly atmospheric sites everywhere in the world; only the most accessible and famous, like Stonehenge, the Pyramids of Gizeh and the Parthenon are under so much pressure from tourism that photography is restricted.

Nevertheless, access is usually the first consideration if you are planning to photograph an archaeological site. There are nearly always some restrictions placed on entry (and an entry fee), to protect delicate monuments. Check these carefully before going, particularly opening and closing times, if any – you may want to shoot at sunrise or sunset, but not all monuments are open to the public at these times. In addition, find out if there are extra fees for photography. This varies from place to place, but in general you are more likely to be charged if you appear to be a professional photographer – a tripod or large camera are often considered indicators of this. Light-sensitive artefacts, such as polychrome murals, may be off-limits for photography, and exhibits in museums usually are. Even if museum photography is permitted, you would need permission to use the photographs (see page 167).

◀ *Timing The location of many ancient monuments is determined by ritual. Khmer temples generally face east – making sunrise the obvious time to shoot (left).*

▶ *Sculpting with light One of the famous face-towers of the Bayon temple at Angkor, Cambodia (right). In late afternoon, the sun highlighted just this face. The angle and lens (180mm) were carefully chosen so that nothing but stone would appear in frame.*

Monuments and public-access sites housing artefacts benefit from not having people in view, but with a large monument this is rare. The best opportunities are nearly always as soon as the site opens.

For atmospheric shots, treat the site as you would a landscape, and try to plan the photography for interesting light – at either end of the day, or possibly with storm clouds. Also look for wide-angle views that take in close details such as a fragment of sculpture, as well as the distance.

INTERIORS

Interior space Whatever kind of room you are faced with, first choose the viewpoint. One of the features of most interiors is that they have more detail than you can take in at a single glance. In order to get a proper sense of the room, you will almost certainly need a wide-angle lens, and a camera position that takes in as much as possible – normally a corner. Most domestic interiors have relatively low ceilings, and a horizontal format is usually the most appropriate. When a room has definite vertical interest – pillars, a chandelier, or ceiling decorations, for example – then consider shooting vertically. Many churches, atriums and other public interiors are like this.

Before committing yourself to one camera position and format, experiment by walking around and trying different compositions in the viewfinder. As with exterior shots of buildings, keep the verticals vertical, unless you go for an obviously angled shot up to a ceiling or down from a balcony. This is usually much easier inside than out – simply keep the camera aimed horizontally, and shoot close to foreground interest such as a table.

Available lighting The most common light source is natural daylight, and it is quite often the most attractive lighting for a room. In any case, decide first whether your main lighting will be this, or the available artificial lighting (if you decide to light the room yourself, see the following pages). The advantage of using natural daylight through windows is that you are more likely to be able to keep the authentic atmosphere of the interior.

▶ *Adapting to conditions Shooting hand-held in Chartres Cathedral called for a fast film – ISO 400. The limits of operation were already set by the maximum aperture of the 24mm lens (f2) and the slowest reliable shutter speed to avoid camera shake (¹/₃₀sec).*

HINTS & TIPS

If the light from a window falls off strongly across the picture frame, fit a graduated filter on the lens, but rotate it so that it shades in the opposite direction to the light.

The more window space there is, the more even the illumination, but much depends on how the windows are distributed. If all along one wall only, the light will fall off quite sharply. If you shoot with the light, the effect is likely to be straightforward but rather flat. Including some of the window area in shot increases the contrast and can cause some flare, but the result is likely to be more atmospheric. A reasonable compromise is side-lighting, with the main windows on one side of the frame.

On a cloudy day, or with direct or diffuse sunlight, the colour temperature will be close to the 5500 K for which daylight film is balanced. However, if the windows are facing a strong blue sky, away from the sun, the colour temperature will be higher, and you will need a light-balancing filter. Because you will probably need a long exposure to suit the light level and still keep good depth of field, ordinary daylight film may not be the best choice. If you use Type B film with an 85B filter, the daylight will balance perfectly and there will be little or no colour cast from reciprocity failure (see page 59). Type B films are made for long exposures.

If you decide to shoot by the interior's own artificial lighting, read pages 100-101 and check the type of lights fitted. Even if you use Type B film in an interior lit by domestic tungsten, the colour will appear fairly orange on film, but may not look unattractive. If you wait until evening, when the room lights are stronger than the light through the windows, the combination can be appealing – the dark blue of dusk and the orange of the room lights.

◀ ▲ *Adjusting exposure Large bright areas in stained-glass windows may need slight over-exposure, although this shot (above) was metered as normal. In low interior light levels, you can use a tripod and a slow shutter speed, as for the interior of this Byzantine church (left), shot when the people were relatively still.*

Adding light There are basically two ways of using photographic lights in an interior – to add to and improve the available lighting, and to create a complete lighting effect from scratch. Think twice before attempting the second option – although it gives you the opportunity to build a lighting set exactly the way you would like it, you will need a number of lights and a lot of time. Also, there is always a danger when you create room lighting that the effect just looks artificial and forced.

In either case, you need to decide what the main light source should be – or appear to be. The choice is usually daylight through windows, or room lights. The simplest way to use photographic lights is to fill in the darker areas of the room. For instance, if you shoot towards a window, it often helps to add light from behind the camera as shadow-fill. On-camera flash is not really satisfactory for this, as it offers too little control and the shadows it casts will be very obvious. Much better is a mains-powered light bounced off part of the walls or ceiling. In many ways, a 3200 K tungsten light is the easiest to use,

BASIC PROCEDURE

- Decide on the viewpoint and lens; set up the camera on a tripod.
- Change the layout of the furniture if necessary to improve the composition. Make sure that everything visible is tidy.
- Choose the main light source and set up additional lights as necessary to balance lighting.
- Check all necessary filters are in place – over lights and lens.
- Bracket exposures when you shoot.

▶ *Minimum lighting For this early morning view in Thomas Jefferson's Monticello (right), fill-in lighting was added to light left-facing shadows. A single 1000-watt quartz lamp, fitted with a blue gel to match the daylight colour temperature, was bounced off the rear wall left of camera.*

▶▶ *Full lighting A hallway gets bright, open treatment (far right) from a combination of two bounced 800-watt lamps (in the corridor beyond and behind the camera) and a ceiling-mounted spot.*

because you can judge the exact balance for yourself. If you are using daylight as the main source, fit a full blue gel over the tungsten light to match it.

Another way of adding photographic lighting is to boost the available light, which may not be enough for good depth of field. Or, if the weather is dull, aiming a light from outside a window (you'll need a long sync lead if you use flash) can simulate sunlight – adjusting the height of the lamp and its colour (with a filter) lets you choose the supposed time of day.

Completely created lighting is a more serious proposition, but sometimes necessary. If you want to simulate daylight, place the main lights outside the windows, as above, but also consider diffusing them with scrim or some other translucent material taped over the windows. This avoids unrealistic multiple shadows. Remember that the aim of lighting an interior is not to illuminate every corner, but to enhance the room's atmosphere. Build up the lighting one step at a time, and as much as possible avoid strong shadows that 'point' to a light source.

Capturing atmosphere To make a really good landscape photograph as opposed to a workmanlike record, it is important to be able to appreciate the complexity of the landscape itself. Most create a wide variety of impressions, from the quality of the lighting and the sense of space to the details of rocks and plants. The essence of most landscape photography is to distil one image from the total of sensory impressions.

Although there are many approaches that you can take, most fall into one of three types. The first is representational, which is essentially a realistic, straightforward treatment. The second is impressionistic, which has much in common with the aims of the French Impressionist painters, suppressing some

▲ **Early light** *Morning mist over the River Stour, Suffolk, with a lone willow (top).*

▲ **Foreground detail** *Olive grove in Tuscany, shot with a 20mm lens stopped down for good depth of field and used close to the ground to emphasize the flowers (above).*

◄ **Open space** *Late afternoon on the coast near Seattle (left) – an uncluttered composition describes space and solitude.*

of the obvious detail in favour of a more atmospheric and evocative image. The third explores the graphic possibilities, also at the expense of recording all the details. In practice, these approaches are often combined.

Light probably makes the biggest difference of all to the mood. As it never remains the same, because of the sun's angle and the weather, the landscape itself is also in a constant state of change. It is often the lighting that suggests a photograph, but you can also, with experience, anticipate it. When you come across a possibly interesting view for the first time, think about whether it would look better at a different time of day. Early and late are often the most interesting times, because the light changes more quickly.

LANDSCAPES

Focal length Landscapes are among the most amenable of all subjects in photography – they can be treated in almost any style imaginable, and with any lens. The character of each focal length has an important effect on the way you deal with a landscape, and the major difference is, naturally enough, between wide-angle and telephoto views.

Wide-angle lenses play two rôles in landscape photography. The first is the all-embracing view. From an overlook, or some other open viewpoint, they give a broad, sweeping view with something of the feeling of a panorama. Depth of field doesn't apply – these are distant views, taking in a large part of the horizon. The other rôle is in bringing a strong sense of depth to a scene by including the close foreground. Details of the landscape, such as flowers, rocks, grass, are juxtaposed with the distant large-scale features and the success of this approach depends on how well you set up the relationship between near and far. The camera position usually has to be quite low, and the aperture very small to ensure great depth of field.

Spatial contrast With a telephoto lens you can select and isolate images from the scene in front of you, and this multiplies your options. From one reasonable viewpoint, you could expect at the most two distinct wide-angle

▲ *Framing a landscape view* Three different focal lengths used from the same camera position, from extreme wide-angle to long telephoto. Although the elements of the landscape are essentially the same in each case, the treatment differs. In particular, the framing needed to be altered: for the 20mm shot (above left), prominence was given to the foreground to give a feeling of depth to the image – looking through from one part of the landscape to another.

The more concentrated 105mm photograph (above centre) also makes use of a rocky outcrop, but at a distance – for this, a tripod and slow shutter speed were necessary so that the lens could be stopped down to f22 for full depth of field. The third shot was taken with a 400mm lens, also on a tripod, framed vertically (above right) to give a sense of the steep hillside rising above the village, and the church catching the first rays of the sun.

views, but you have several choices with a telephoto lens. The longer the lens, the greater the selectivity. The wide-angle possibilities are usually obvious as soon as you reach a viewpoint, but the longer, cropped-in views may take time to discover. The way in which telephotos compress perspective (see pages 52-53) works particularly well in landscapes that have strong relief, such as a series of ranges of hills stretching away to the horizon. In a case like this, the different distances appear like stacked planes.

Long lenses outdoors need some care in use – you need to consider the practicalities of working in an exposed location. A tripod helps composition and reduces the risk of camera shake, but may be no protection against a breeze. On a windy day, shelter the lens and tripod, or at least shoot from a low position.

LANDSCAPES

▲ *Emerging light* Overcast clearing slowly over Mount Rainier, Washington – *photographed with a 2-stop graduated filter to balance sky and landscape.*

A feeling for weather Weather is all-important to landscapes. It controls the way the light strikes, from the soft raking sunlight of a hazy autumnal morning to a flat grey overcast. If you take a serious approach to photographing landscapes, it means that you should be prepared for two things: to anticipate what the weather will be like so that you can plan a shot in advance, and to be able to appreciate and exploit any unexpected changes in the weather.

Knowing the likely conditions in a given location can give you the chance to reorganize an itinerary so that, for instance, you can arrange to be in position for a clear sunset where you need one, or a storm over a dramatic setting.

Britain, for example, gets most of its weather from a string of depressions crossing the Atlantic. Fronts mark the changes between the cold air and warm air that move around these depressions – there is likely to be a clear, bright period behind a cold front, in contrast to the slow, grey passage of a warm front. Fine, stable weather usually comes with a mass of high-pressure air that diverts the depressions – more common in summer than winter.

When you are travelling, weather conditions may not be at all like those at home, so again it pays to find out in advance, so you know what kind of weather to expect. It is, after all, part of the essence of a particular landscape.

▲ Hazy sunrise *Morning mist is common over low-lying wetlands, as in this riverside view in Dedham Vale (above).*

◀ Colours in weather *Tropical haze produces pastel colours, weak sun and strong aerial perspective over the Mekong River in Laos (left).*

◀ Changing conditions *Clouds swirl over Kelimutu volcano on the Indonesian island of Flores (left), clearing in patches for a few minutes at a time – this characteristic mountain weather gives a constantly changing view.*

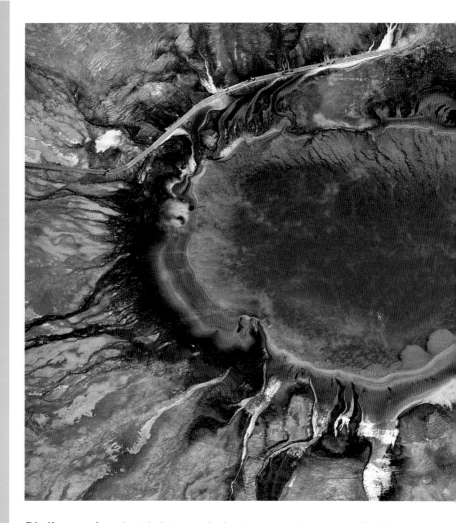

Bird's-eye view Aerial photography has its own unique range of subjects and styles of picture, particularly if you shoot vertically downwards for what can be unusual, abstract images. Patterns that are invisible on the ground can be the most striking part of an aerial photograph.

The single most important factor that separates ordinary from good aerial photographs is the lighting. Direct sunlight is almost always better than an overcast day – the contrast is higher and, being brighter, allows higher shutter speeds. A high sun in the middle of the day, however, tends to give flat lighting – even more apparent if you are shooting vertically downwards rather than obliquely. More reliably attractive is a low sun in the early morning and late afternoon; this casts longer shadows and gives a stronger and better defined

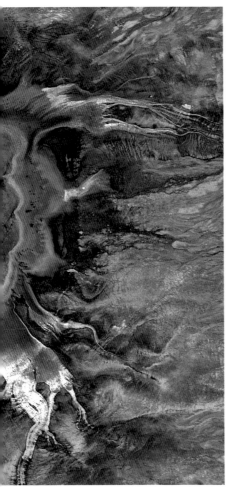

▲ *Dramatic lighting* Sunlight under storm clouds, reflected in a river (above).

◄ *Unique effects* In the Grand Prismatic Spring, Yellowstone, algae in the warm water create the colours (left). Both these shots used a 180mm lens and ISO 64 film at ¹/₅₀₀ sec, f2.8.

image. One of aerial photography's special problems is haze, because of the thickness of the atmosphere that you have to shoot through. The simplest solution is to fly low – say, about 1000 feet (305 metres) above ground level – and use a wide-angle lens. A UV filter or, stronger still, a polarizing filter, also helps sharpen contrast and cut through atmospheric haze.

Practicalities The most useful aircraft is usually a single-engined, high-winged plane, such as a Cessna. Flying time is relatively inexpensive, the aircraft is highly manoeuvrable, and the view unrestricted by the wings. From either door, the angle of view from wing tip to wheel is just sufficient for a 20mm or 24mm lens to be used on a 35mm camera.

Larger, low-winged aircraft offer very limited visibility, and almost the only possibility for a clear view is to use the rear luggage hatch (which has to be removed), which guarantees an uncomfortable flight. Helicopters have wonderful manouevrability, but are much more expensive. Avoid including the rotor blades in frame – although they appear blurred to the eye, a high shutter speed will record them on film quite clearly and spoil the shot.

Angle of view Normal level flight allows only diagonal shooting at a shallow angle, which works well for distant scenic views. For close, graphic shots, however, a steeper shooting angle is usually better. For this, the aircraft must be banked, and as this puts it into a turn, shooting may be limited to just a few seconds. One alternative is to slip the aircraft sideways towards the subject, reducing the throttle to dampen vibration. Another is to fly in a tight circle over the subject (but make sure that the circle is centred on the subject, not the aircraft). Never shoot through aircraft windows if you can help it.

HINTS & TIPS

For sharper, clearer pictures:
* *Fly low – the less atmosphere between you and the ground, the better*
* *Use a wide-angle lens to make haze less obvious*
* *Use a UV or polarizing filter: both cut down UV scattering; a polarizing filter reduces reflections from the atmosphere*
* *Shoot away from the sun, which reduces back-scattering from haze*
* *Do not over-expose slides – saturated images look clearer*

However clean and unscratched (rare in any case), a window reduces sharpness and adds a slight flare. If you cannot avoid it, keep the camera as close to the plastic as possible, and use a piece of cloth or your hands to eliminate reflections. Do not shoot when sunlight strikes the window, causing flare and showing up any scratches on the perspex. Avoid transmitting vibration to the camera by not resting your arm or the camera on any part of the aircraft body. Also, do not lean out of the aircraft – the airflow may tear the camera from your hands, quite apart from the other, more obvious, dangers.

As on the ground, different focal lengths of lens give different types of image. Wide-angle lenses are particularly good for overall views with less haze (see above). The standard focal length of around 50mm is obviously useful for most subjects, while a moderate telephoto (but nothing more than 200mm) can be used to pick out smaller subjects, like a flock of birds. Keep the aperture wide open and set the highest shutter speed possible (at least $^1/_{250}$ sec, but better $^1/_{500}$) to avoid camera shake. Take care with the focus when you use a telephoto lens – if you are flying at one or two thousand feet, the ground will not quite be in focus if the the lens setting is at infinity.

PREPARING FOR THE FLIGHT

Planning ahead saves time and money — both important in aerial photography. Follow this checklist before take-off:

Plan the route Use a map — an aeronautical one if possible — and mark on it the locations that interest you. If there is any uncertainty, make up a list of the types of subject. Check with the pilot what the ground speed will be at the height at which you plan to shoot, and calculate the flight time.

Choose the time of day Check the weather reports — and their reliability. Double-check by enquiring at the airfield. Allow about half an hour before take-off to prepare equipment and the aircraft.

Brief the pilot Explain the subjects you plan to shoot, and whether you want a vertical or diagonal view. Agree procedures for banking and changing altitude.

Prepare the aircraft Tell the pilot beforehand that you will need a clear view. Adjust the seating if necessary, check the field of view, and install the camera case so that equipment and film are easily accessible.

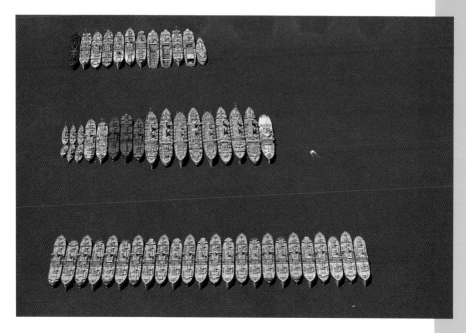

▲ **Discovering a pattern** *The aerial view reveals an abstract pattern of repeated shapes formed by 'mothballed' naval vessels lying up near San Francisco.*

ANIMALS

▲ *Close-up A young orang-utan's experiments with plumbing in a zoo (above) make a good opportunity for a portrait.*

◀ *Locating the subject During the heat of the day, young water monitors in India often make for the trees (left). Knowing behaviour patterns like this improves the chances of finding animals.*

Location There is a big difference in technique and in the level of difficulty between photographing animals in captivity and those in the wild. Many modern zoos allow animals to behave in an approximately natural way, and usually offer some good oportunities for close-ups and animal portraits. Nothing, however, comes close to photographing animals in their natural habitat.

Wildlife photography relies heavily on fieldcraft – finding the animal and a suitable position for shooting, in most cases unobserved. Whatever the subject, improve your chances of success by spending time in advance on research and planning. The first step is to find a good location. Established wildlife reserves and national parks are often the best places. Make sure that you visit at the best time of year for seeing the animals – this varies between places and species.

Basic equipment includes at least one telephoto lens. A medium telephoto is useful for stalking and for medium-to-large animals that are safe to approach, but the most useful lens by far is a long, and ideally fast, telephoto of at least 400mm. 600mm is even better, although good lenses of these focal lengths are unavoidably expensive. Many animals are at their most active around dawn and dusk, which means working in low light levels; this in turn puts a premium on a wide maximum aperture (more expensive still) and may call for a change to a faster film. Standard lenses are more useful for remote-control photography, in which the camera is set up at close range, often with flash attached; but this is a highly specialized technique.

BIRDS IN FLIGHT

Birds make good, active subjects for the camera when they are flying, but this calls for very good technique. The two major problems are focus and exposure. A fast-reacting auto-focus system is a definite advantage, but the speed of approach can sometimes be too fast. First, position yourself close to a known flight path. One of the most reliable is near a nesting colony at the time when the birds are collecting materials for nest-building.

With a manually-focused lens, there are three ways of focusing on a bird flying towards you:

Fixed focus Focus ahead of the bird (easy if there is a regular flight path) and wait for it to fly into focus.

Follow-focus Focus on the bird as soon as you see it, and turn the focusing ring to keep pace with it. In theory this gives several shooting opportunities, but in practice it is very difficult to maintain sharp focus.

▲ *Single subject Open-billed stork bringing nesting materials to the winter colony, shot with 600mm lens, $^1/_{250}$ sec, f5.6.*

Continuous re-focusing This is a mixture of the first two techniques. Focus more or less on the bird, and then quickly shift the focus a little ahead of it and wait for it to fly into focus. Shoot and re-focus ahead of the bird, and so on. If the bird is against a normal blue sky, the camera's metering system will usually work well. Against a light cloudy sky, however, you may need to increase the exposure up to two stops beyond the meter reading. Against a deep blue sky or dark storm-clouds, you may need to reduce the exposure.

ANIMALS

Fieldcraft The two basic techniques are stalking and photographing from a hide. Stalking needs less preparation but more fieldcraft, and the chances of success are rarely high. In many ways, you will need to use the techniques in which animals themselves hunt or avoid being hunted. Take the minimum of equipment, and carry the camera, with telephoto lens fitted, ready for instant shooting – encounters often happen unexpectedly.

STALKING TECHNIQUES

• Use camouflage or drab clothing and tape over chrome fittings on the cameras.
• Minimize your odour by wearing no deodorant, being well clothed, and staying downwind of the animal.
• Move quietly and smoothly and carry nothing that rattles.
• Stay close to cover and in the shade wherever possible.
• If seen, freeze and stay motionless until the animal relaxes. Avoid any eye contact.

▲ *Animal activity* Normal behaviour patterns offer very different moods, such as the drama of spotted deer fighting at Wilpattu National Park, Sri Lanka (top), contrasted with the calm domesticity of Indian elephants with their young (above).

The alternative to stalking is to use a hide, also called a blind. This is a concealed camera position usually sited inside the animal's territory, and allows closer shooting than would be possible if you were exposed to view. It is often the only practical method. If you have no experience of constructing a hide and moving it close into position, it is best to work from a permanent hide that has been established in a wildlife reserve.

HINTS & TIPS

Move into a hide when the animal is away (such as during a food-gathering session). If you have been spotted entering, you may have to wait some time for the animals to settle down. Once inside, stay quiet and move as little as possible.

▲ *The right location In grassland, such as this East African reserve at Lake Mayara, vehicles function as hides – the animals are accustomed to them. Hippo pools usually have plenty of activity, and it is worth waiting for moments like this.*

A well-sited hide is set up in a way that makes it comfortable enough to spend some hours at a time in, and is in direct line of sight to a known place that the animals visit regularly – such as a nest or lair, or where the animals feed, drink or bathe. For photography, the position of the sun in relation to the view and the camera is important, as is an entrance that is hidden from the animals' view.

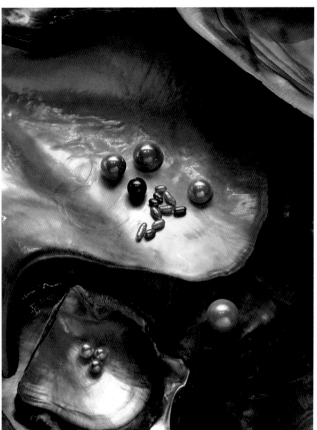

Composed and found images The tradition of still life in painting is continued in photography. The still-life image is one of the mainstays of studio photography, but there are also infinite possibilities for finding subjects in real life. The most successful images are usually those in which the photographer explores the physical nature of objects – their texture, volume, colour, arrangement and relationships with other objects. This makes the design of the photograph extremely important, and the lighting.

A special feature of still-life photography is that you can exercise total control over the image. Indeed, if you are arranging a still-life set in a studio or at home, the entire concept of the image, from finding the subject through to lighting it is in your hands. This contrasts with most kinds of photography, in which you are recording and interpreting scenes as you find them.

Most still-life images start with an object, or group of objects, that for one reason or another appeals to the photographer. The important things to

◄◄ *Surface values* Controlled lighting and painstaking arrangement are the hallmarks of a classic studio still life, here different kinds of pearls on oyster shells (far left). Diffused directional lighting captures the volume of objects and the iridescent sheen characteristic of pearl and mother-of-pearl.

◄ *Natural texture* A bolt in a knot of old wood (left) makes a found still-life with texture as the main appeal, brought out by bright sunlight striking at a raking angle.

REFLECTIVE OBJECTS

Shiny surfaces like polished metal or glass need special lighting treatment – a spotlight, for instance, will simply create a hot-spot. The essential thing to remember is that this kind of object reflects the light source. The normal treatment is to make the light source large and even enough so that its reflection covers all of the subject. You can use a soft-box diffuser, or bounce the light off a white wall or white paper. A special version of this diffusion is a light-tent – a continuous sheet of material, like tracing paper, wrapped around the scene; the lights are aimed through from outside, with just a small hole left for the camera lens.

decide are the angle of view (especially with a single object in close-up), the setting (including the background and other objects), the composition, and lighting. The last is in many ways the critical element in a still life – the scale of most sets means that you have great freedom in how you light them. Don't limit your ideas simply to showing an object efficiently; experiment with light.

BACKGROUNDS

If you have a single object, or a small group, to photograph, you will normally have to choose the setting. Look for a surface and back-drop that will complement the subject visually and provide a relevant background, such as a kitchen work-top for a food shot. Commonly used backgrounds include white Formica, black velvet, backlit translucent plastic, glass, stone, textured paper.

▶ **CLOSE-UP**

▲ ***Ring flash*** *This is a device specially designed for efficient close-up photography in cramped spaces. Because the flash tube surrounds the front of the lens, the lighting is absolutely shadowless, as in this magnified view of a flower stamen.*

The unusual view Close-up photography has a tremendous capacity for producing unexpected images. You can use framing, focus and depth of field with great precision to isolate special details – even more than at normal scales. Lenses of all kinds focus more closely when they are moved away from the film. At distances of less than a few inches, the movement is considerable, and so usually needs either a special lens or special attachments. The point at which close-up photography diverges from normal scales is a magnification of about one seventh. Depth of field becomes shallower the closer a lens focuses, and this strongly influences the character of macro images – it is easy to isolate subjects, but often difficult to get sharpness across the frame. Use a small aperture and position the camera face on to the shallowest plane of a subject.

CLOSE FOCUSING MECHANISMS

Extension rings *(left) The simplest and sturdiest way of increasing the distance between lens and film is to fit a ring beween the lens and the camera body. These are available in different thicknesses, and can be added together. The lens can still be focused within a small range. An extension ring, or set, that has the same thickness as the lens focal length doubles the magnification. In other words, if you extend a 50mm lens by another 50mm, the magnification will be 1x (life-size).*

Supplementary close-up lenses *These are simple one-element lenses that fit in front of the lens like a filter. They give modest magnification, but a slight loss of picture quality. Their advantage is that they are easy and quick to fit.*

Reverse the lens *At magnifications greater than 1x, most lenses perform better optically if they are turned round. A reversing ring does this for certain makes of equipment.*

1x

Extension bellows *(left) These are flexible versions of extension rings, and can be adjusted to any extension up to their limit. They are useful for extreme close-ups, but may need a double cable release to keep the aperture working automatically.*

Macro lens *The optics on most lenses are designed to work at their peak at normal distances (several feet to infinity). A macro lens gives its sharpest images in close-up. 'Macro-focusing' lenses are basically regular lenses with an extended focusing mechanism.*

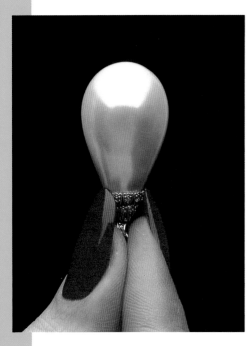

◀ *Surface texture* The pearl (the largest known gem-quality natural pearl) needed soft lighting for its reflective surface, but not so even that the shape and sheen were lost. A soft-box fitted to a flash unit was suspended overhead, with pieces of white card on either side as reflectors. Flash was essential to freeze any movement of the hand (left).

▶ *Clarity* Natural daylight on a cloudy day gave very diffused lighting that helped to keep this shot of a damsel fly (right) simple and delicate. The depth of field was limited by the light level and a shutter speed of $^1/_4$ sec (the camera mounted on a tripod) to f16. To make sure that all of the insect was sharply focused, the 200mm macro lens was positioned exactly side-on to the fly.

Close-up exposure As the usual way of magnifying an image is to move the lens away from the film (which happens even with a macro lens), this affects the exposure. More light is needed to give a good exposure, and this means a wider aperture, or a slower shutter speed, or adding more light from a flash. Fortunately, modern automatic cameras generally take care of all this, but with a non-automatic camera you need to work out the new settings for yourself. Focus on the scale below and read off the extra exposure needed, as explained opposite. Use this method only if your camera does not measure the exposure automatically.

Close-up lighting At these small scales, ordinary lighting tends to look more diffuse, and sometimes flat. With some subjects this is a help, but to create a more normal contrast, use an additional light source, such as a small flash unit. Match this with a similarly miniature set of reflectors, such as small scraps of card and foil, and small mirrors (dental mirrors are the best). Flash is

f. stop increase

4   3   2   1$^2/_3$ 1$^1/_3$ 1   2$_f$

absolutely necessary for moving subjects such as insects, and generally produces a crisper and more colourful image – use it off the camera and close to the subject to avoid shadows from the front of the lens. The bigger the lens extension, the more light is needed – it is a great advantage to use a flash unit that allows the camera's meter to continue working automatically.

Close-up exposure scale *The scale along the bottom of these pages works for 35mm SLR cameras. At whatever magnification and focus setting you intend to shoot, aim the camera at this scale so that the large arrow is at one end of the frame and in sharp focus (move the camera in and out). The last figure that you can see on the right through the viewfinder is the amount by which you increase your f-stop setting.*

¹/₃
▼

Capturing the exotic Exotic is a relative term: it depends on who is taking the photographs, and who is looking at them. It has to do with scenes and atmospheres that are unfamiliar to you as photographer, even though they may be unremarkable to the local population. The essence of travel photography is to get across your enthusiasm in seeing new places, people and things, observing both the overall impression and the descriptive detail.

However, do not forget that when travelling, you are the outsider; there is an etiquette to be observed. Forbidden and disapproved subjects vary from country to country and you should check that, for example, it is acceptable to photograph religious sites. Conditions of poverty can produce surprisingly

▲ *Special events* November full-moon festival with fireworks over a chedi in northern Thailand.

◀ *Descriptive detail* Close-up of gilded door panels in a Laotian temple.

HINTS & TIPS

For a quick preview of the local sights, take a look at the postcard rack at the airport or hotel. Avoid copying the views, although this may be difficult as local postcard photographers usually know the best viewpoints; but use the pictures for information about lighting.

impactful pictures, but this is an increasingly sensitive issue, clearly open to interpretation. It is worth exercising both courtesy and caution when approaching human subjects whose way of life is very different from your own.

On a foreign trip, you will probably be photographing intensely and taking in a great variety of information. The experiences may be vividly etched in your mind, but it is easy to forget exact times and places after you have returned home and had your films processed. Carry a notebook with you on your travels and record, at least approximately, the subjects and locations as you find them, so you can later catalogue your pictures accurately.

Preparations When travelling, you will have no problem finding interesting locations and events to shoot. Successful photography depends as much on safeguarding your equipment as you travel and being aware of the special problems of transporting valuable technical items.

Packing Take special care over how you pack your equipment for travelling. Although most modern 35mm cameras are robust, they are still more fragile than most normal luggage, and need to be protected from knocks, vibration, water and dust.

Insurance Special policies are available for photographic equipment. Make sure that you insure what you need for where you intend to use it. List all the items over the minimum amount with serial numbers if they have them. List the replacement value, not the cost if they are old – and up-date the prices each year. Read the exclusions on the policy.

Customs If you carry only a modest amount of equipment, you should have no special difficulties, but it is always a good idea to carry copies of receipts, so that you can prove that the equipment belongs to you and you have already paid duty on it.

X-rays X-ray inspections are an inevitable part of air travel. Almost every airport has the machines, and using them for carry-on baggage at least is standard procedure. There are just three important facts for photographers:
● X-rays have a cumulative effect – it builds up with the number of doses.
● In principle, they fog film in much the same way as does light. Like light, they affect fast films more readily than slow films.
● The dose from a modern airport machine is far too small to have any noticeable effect.
    In other words, if you are travelling with ordinary film and flying directly to your destination from a fairly modern airport, the X-ray machine will have no measurable effect. If you are changing planes and airports a number of times on a trip, however, then you may have some reason to worry. In the US, you are entitled to a hand-search instead of X-ray inspection under their flying regulations. It will improve your chances of being given a hand inspection if the film is easy to see – in clear containers and a clear plastic bag.

Processing abroad One answer to the airport X-ray problem is to buy and process your films on location. The E-6 process for colour slides and C-41 for colour negatives are nearly universal. If you are using Kodachrome, however, there is only a small choice of labs. If you plan to buy film abroad, check in advance that you can buy the type you want.

Electrical supply More and more photographic equipment needs electrical power, some of it direct from the mains, some from re-chargeable batteries. Voltages are usually either 110/120v or 220/240v. The list below shows where. The cycles (50 or 60 Hz) only matter for rotating components, and have no effect on lights or chargers. Carry a plug adapter or buy plugs locally.

110/120v	220/240v	
Barbados	Algeria	Kuwait
Bermuda	Andorra	Laos
Canada	Argentina	Latvia
Cayman Islands	Australia	Lebanon (also 110v)
Colombia	(240-250v)	Lithuania
Cuba	Austria	Luxembourg
Ecuador	Belgium	Malaysia
El Salvador	Bosnia	Malta
Guam	Brazil (Rio 120v)	Monaco
Guatemala	Brunei (230v)	Morocco
Honduras (also 220v)	Bulgaria	Nepal
Jamaica	Burma	Netherlands
Japan (100v)	Cambodia	New Zealand (230v)
Jordan (also 220v)	Chile	Norway
Korea (S. and N., also 220v)	China	Pakistan
Lebanon (also 220v)	C.I.S.	Paraguay
Mexico	Croatia	Peru
Nicaragua	Cyprus	Philippines
Panama	Czech Republic	Poland
Puerto Rico	Denmark	Portugal
Saudi Arabia (also 220v)	Egypt	Romania
Taiwan	Estonia	San Marino
Trinidad	Fiji	Saudi Arabia (also 110v)
USA	Finland	Senegal
Venezuela (also 220v)	France	Serbia
	Germany	Singapore
	Greece	Slovak Republic
	Haiti	South Africa (220-230v)
	Hong Kong	Spain (also 110v)
	(200v)	Sri Lanka
	Hungary	Sweden
	India	Switzerland
	Indonesia	Tanzania
	Iran	Thailand
	Ireland	Tunisia (also 110v)
	Israel	Turkey
	Italy	UK
	Jordan (also 110v)	Uruguay
	Kenya	Vietnam (also 110v)

Slide mounts For protection and display, mount 35mm slides. Processing laboratories will do this, but it may be cheaper and more efficient to buy and use your own mounts. Slide mounts are available in card, plastic or metal, with and without glass. The advantages of card mounts, particularly heat-sealed ones which are unlikely to come apart with age, are that they are inexpensive and you can write information on them very easily. If you shoot a sufficient quantity of film, consider ordering a few thousand mounts at a time and having them custom-printed with your name and copyright symbol ©. Glass (in plastic and metal mounts only) in theory protects the emulsion, but it can also trap dirt and cause scratching. For storage, a simple clear acetate cover that slips over each slide mount is adequate. Medium- and large-format transparencies can be kept in individual sleeves (or card, plastic or metal mounts for medium-format).

▲ *Filing drawers Large filing cabinets accommodate slides fitted into plastic view-sheets, which enables you to file sets under subject or location.*

▲ *Trays Shallow trays hold the slides packed in rows. It is less easy to find what you need, as you have to remove and look at each one separately.*

Storing slides and negatives Use only archival materials that cannot damage your pictures – wood, for instance, and some glues, release gases that will damage emulsions over time. In practice, this means buying well-known brands of purpose-made mounting and filing products. 35mm slides can be kept in plastic sheets with pockets that hold typically 20 at a time – these are easy to view, and can be filed in trays or inside ring-bound covers, or hung on racks in a cabinet file. Roll-film slides can be kept in the same way. A more compact way of storing slides is stacked together in shallow trays or boxes, but it is less easy to look through them. Negatives are usually best kept in strips of six (for 35mm film) in purpose-made acetate sheets that each hold one roll of film. These can be kept all together in a drawer or file.

Light boxes Although slides look their most spectacular when projected on a screen, a light box is far more useful for sorting, editing and examining them. A sheet of 36 uncut 35mm frames will fit on a 12x10 inch (30x25 cm) light box; 36 mounted frames need a slightly larger area – 12x12 inches (30x30 cm). In fact, though, for editing it is better to have more room than this for grouping and rearranging.

▲ *Loupes There are various types of magnifier that you can use to view slides in close-up on a light box. Choose the size, magnification strength and accuracy of the loupe according to what you need.*

Slide projectors A good-quality slide projector makes the most of the brightness and richness of a colour transparency. The most important qualities to look for are the basic ones of lens (good optics), the arrangement of lamp and fan (bright but not likely to over-heat the slide), and a mechanically sound feeder system. Carousel slide projectors are almost an industry standard: the horizontal circular trays hold 80 slide mounts and work by simple gravity feed. A remote-control handset allows forward and backward changes, and focus control. Useful refinements are a zoom lens, which allows you to fill the screen exactly whatever the distance, and automatic focus.

A step beyond a single slide projector is to link two together with a fade control. Mount the slides for a presentation alternately in the two carousels, and the system presents them in an uninterrupted sequence, dissolving from one image to the next by dimming and brightening the lamps. For professional multi-vision slide presentations, a number of projectors can be linked, and the images projected on different screens (or different areas of one large screen). The rates of change from one image to the next can be varied, and the entire programme can be worked out in advance and operated by computer.

Video imagers Using imaging chips similar to those in camcorders, these machines display slides on an ordinary television monitor. Brightness, colour and enlargement can usually all be controlled on the machine. The image quality is not as high as in normal slide projection, but the viewing method is extremely convenient. For the next step up in electronic imaging, see the following pages.

Photo CD *Kodak's Photo CD system is an industry standard for storing images digitally, and can be used with other imaging software. You take a number of slides or negatives to a photo finishing lab, where they are transferred onto an unerasable CD. The CD is then an electronic picture file that can be used for printing, viewing, and changing images.*

Image scanning Although photography relies almost totally on film, there are more and more reasons for storing the images digitally. Indeed, all the pictures in this book, as in most other publications, have been scanned digitally so that they can be printed on the page. The new generation of film labs that make regular photographic prints from your negatives and slides also digitize the images first. If you have a suitable computer and the right software, you can scan your photographs and manipulate them to any degree you like. The opportunities for doing more to the image on a computer are special and almost without limit.

▲ *Computer image This was scanned onto Kodak Photo CD, and displayed on a monitor in Adobe Photoshop.*

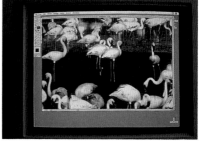

▲ *Image amendment Using the zoom control, small areas of the image can be enlarged and retouched.*

When a photograph is scanned, the image is divided into a large number of regularly spaced rectangles, called pixels. Each one has a value – in tone and colour. Provided that they are small enough, they cannot be seen individually, and the whole image looks continuous. To the eye, this is not so different from the way film grain works – an ordinary photograph looks seamless at a normal viewing distance, but if you take a magnifier loupe to it, the image breaks up into clumps of grain. The image quality in a digital picture depends very much on the number of pixels packed into it – the more pixels, the better the detail, just as a fine-grain film gives the sharpest photographs.

Scanning to the best resolution possible is slow and expensive, particularly in colour, which needs several kinds of information for each pixel. Lasers resolve more detail than a lens, and the large number of pixels (10 million or more for a high-quality scan of a 35mm frame) needs hardware and software with a big storage capacity.

Even a moderately detailed image needs a lot of storage space – more than a floppy disk has. Professionally, digital images are stored on tape and on removable hard disks, but CDs are becoming widely used. Kodak's Photo CD system can store up to 100 images at quite high resolution.

▲ **Digitizing** *Digitized photographs can be manipulated with a computer in many ways, to produce images a long way from* *reality. Computer manipulation was used at all stages of this picture showing production of a digital humming bird.*

PIXELS, RESOLUTION AND FILE SIZE

The higher the resolution that you want, the more pixels you need. A 35mm colour image made up of 1 million pixels measures about 3800 x 2500 pixels but needs 3 megabytes (MB) of storage space. 5 million pixels take up 15 MB, and so on. To make large files manageable, some software compresses the information. Some image compression loses detail, other methods preserve it by cutting out repetition.

COMPUTER MANIPULATION

Equipment Once you have a digitized photograph, in principle you can do almost anything with it. You need a computer with a hard disk, enough memory to handle the image file and a fairly fast processor, but a mid-range desktop computer will normally be up to the job. Your screen and display adapter must be able to handle 24-bit colour bit-mapped images. Apart from these, you will need appropriate software, such as Adobe Photoshop or ColorStudio. Imaging software like these overcomes the problem of working with big, multi-megabyte files by taking over part of your computer's hard disk and using it as memory. This process, known as virtual memory, makes it possible to work on, say, an 18 MB image with as little as 2 MB RAM (random access memory). Nevertheless, the more memory (RAM) you have the better – 4 MB, 8 MB or even more.

▲ *Reworking A basic set of imaging controls allows contrast, brightness and colour to be altered. In Adobe Photoshop, simple slider controls are operated by the cursor (using a mouse or stylus), and the screen gives a preview of the effect.*

IMAGING TOOLS

The menu of tools for selecting and manipulating the image varies between software makes, but most offer a similar choice.

Selection: The basic tool is a mask that you make by drawing an outline around part of the image. One option is a feather edge for seamless blending. Another method of selection is automatic, by tone or colour.

Adjustment: You can change all the image qualities as you would wish to in a top-quality hand-shaded photo, and with greater control. Adjust brightness, contrast, highlights, shadows, and all the colour qualities (independently for highlights, mid-tones and shadows if necessary).

Filters: These have much the same effect as special effects filters for the camera – blurring, softening, sharpening, sharpening edges, streaking, and various kinds of distortion.

Dynamic effects: Rotate, stretch, flip, slant and bend parts of the image. You can also re-size parts of the image.

Paintbrush: This works like a universal, infinitely adaptable retouching tool that can imitate brush, airbrush, pen and other tools. You can adjust the flow and density of the 'paint'. A useful device is the clone tool, which allows you to paint with another part of the image. This makes it possible to add complex textures such as vegetation, rock or a brick wall very easily.

Cleaning up the image At the simplest level, you can use the computer to tidy up spots and blemishes – rather like spotting a print, but with more facilities and no danger of making an irreversible mistake. A bad processing mark on the film, or the shadow of a hair stuck in the film gate? No problem – retouch it out. You need again never throw away physically damaged slides or negatives. You can take this image-tidying as far as you like, even to removing litter in a foreground.

Altering tones and colours Use the adjustment tools in the software to make changes to the brightness and the colour – overall or selectively. If the contrast is too high, reduce it. Or keep the overall contrast high while expanding the range in the shadows. Tone down the intensity of a blue sky, or neutralize a green cast caused by reciprocity failure in a long exposure.

▶ *Colour correction Part of a sequence of making electronic corrections to a digitized picture. The photograph is a time exposure at night, under moonlight, lasting an hour and a half. Severe reciprocity failure has given an overall green cast, while part of the streak of a star appears in the top left corner. The picture was digitized on Kodak's Photo CD system, and then loaded into Adobe Photoshop for manipulation. The first step was to increase the contrast slightly and lower the brightness (note that the images here were shot off the screen and appear to have more contrast than they really do). The next step was to neutralize the colour cast – by working on individual colours and tones.*

Removing unwanted parts For more serious image surgery, you can take picture elements that you don't like right out of the picture. Use the selection tools to identify them and erase them, and fill in the gap with texture from the background using the clone tool.

Combining images Going a step beyond removing elements, use the cut-and-paste facility to select something in one picture, remove it, and paste it into a second photograph. For example, change the sky by adding a more interesting one from your library of cloud shots. Or simply paste in a few more clouds. You can go even further and construct elaborate special effects shots.

▶ **Erasing** *The star streak was finally wiped out by selecting the 'rubber stamp' tool, and was replaced with a nearby patch of sky.*

REFERENCE SECTION

ESSENTIALS BEFORE SHOOTING

- Check the batteries — make sure they are fresh and working.
- Check the camera is loaded with film.
- Check the correct film speed is set (if not automatic).
- Check that there is no dirt or grease on the lens.
- Have one or more spare rolls of film ready.
- Set the program mode you think you will need (on a fully automatic camera), or a suitable aperture/shutter speed combination (on a semi- or non-automatic model).
- If the camera is automatic, aim it at a typical view and check that the exposure settings are what you would expect them to be.
- Test the auto-focus (if there is one) by aiming and half-pressing the shutter release.

Quick performance check Occasionally do a visual check of the basic camera functions. Also do this if you suspect any problems.
NOTE: Not all of these checks will work with fully automatic cameras.

- Compare meter readings of the same view with another camera or a hand-held meter.

- In the middle of a sunny day, an average subject (neither very bright nor very dark) should give a reading of about f16 at $1/60$ sec with ISO 50 or ISO 64 film, f16 at $1/125$ sec with ISO 100 or ISO 125 film, and so on.

- With the camera on automatic shutter priority, aim it at one view and change the shutter speed from slow to fast. The aperture reading should change by exactly one f-stop each time. If the camera can be set to aperture priority, do the equivalent by changing the aperture one stop at a time.

- Open the camera back and hold the camera pointing away from you against the sky or any bright area. Open the lens aperture fully. Shoot through the range of shutter speeds from the slowest upwards. With a non-reflex camera you should be able to see that the shutter remains open half as long each time. although the fastest settings will be difficult to judge. With an SLR, this happens for the slower speeds, up to about $1/60$ sec. At the faster speeds, the gap between the two shutter curtains gets narrower each time.

- With the camera in the same position, set the shutter to B , press the release and work the aperture control. It should close and open normally.

Rights Photography is an innocent enough activity for most people, but it is as well to know your rights, and what restrictions you might face. There are three areas: taking photographs, ownership and using photographs.

Permission to shoot In a public place you can use a camera as much as you like, providing you do not set up a tripod or other equipment in such a way that you cause an obstruction or a public nuisance. In a private place open to the public (such as museums and even some parks) you have to go by the regulations. In some ways it's better always to ask, but use common-sense as a guide – see if other people are also taking photographs. In private places not open to the public, ask first.

Copyright This is a special version of a property right that applies to authors, and includes photographs. In the UK, it is covered by the Copyright, Designs and Patents Act 1988, which gives you, the photographer, first copyright in your pictures, even if you took them on commission for someone else (unless you took them as part of your employment). Of course, copyright can be assigned, but that is up to you. Copyright remains in the photographer's estate until 50 years after death. You also have Moral Rights to be identified as the author of a photograph, the right to object to any derogatory treatment of it, and the right not to have a photograph falsely attributed to you.

In the US, the matter is covered by the Copyright Act of 1976, which also makes the photographer the owner of the copyright unless the photograph is 'work made for hire' (when the person or company employing the photographer owns the copyright). Unless you register the copyright of a photograph at the US Copyright Office, you have the responsibility of protecting it by making sure that there is a copyright notice on it and wherever published. A copyright notice reads: '© (year) (photographer's name)'; for example, © 1993 Michael Freeman.

Permission to use This depends on what the subject is, and how you use the picture. If you use a photograph of a person for news or educational purposes (for example printed in a magazine article), then there are normally no problems. For advertising and other 'purposes of trade', however, you must definitely have permission. Professional photographers have their subjects sign a model release for this reason. Beware of using pictures taken on private property without permission, not even in Disneyworld (especially not there – the Disney Corporation is well known for taking legal action over the use of pictures of Mickey Mouse et al). Works of art also need permission. In the UK, you can only include copyrighted images (in which are included pictures on a television screen) if they are 'incidental'.

CHECKLISTS

▲

Equipment and subject This chart enables you to check the cameras, film and accessories best suited to particular subjects or essential for certain kinds of photographic work. In the columns reading across the chart, the subjects are coded by letter (see list below). In each column you can see numerical codes aligned with the items on the list of equipment. These tell you the relative importance of each item in relation to the subject, depending on whether they are essential, important to your efficiency and successful results, or merely useful.

KEY TO CODES

A Reportage
B Casual outdoor portrait
C Planned outdoor portrait
D Planned indoor portrait
E Festivals
F Buildings
G Interiors
H Landscapes
I Mountains
J Aerial views
K Animals (stalking)
L Animals (from a hide)
M Still life
N Close-up

1 Essential
2 Important
3 Useful

	A	B
CAMERAS		
COMPACT 35mm	2	2
AUTO-FOCUS COMPACT	2	2
BASIC 35mm SLR	2	2
AUTO-FOCUS SLR	2	2
PANORAMIC		
ROLL-FILM		3
LARGE-FORMAT		
LENSES		
STANDARD	2	2
WIDE-ANGLE	3	3
EXTREME WIDE-ANGLE		
FISHEYE		
MEDIUM TELEPHOTO	2	1
EXTREME TELEPHOTO	3	
WIDE-ANGLE ZOOM	2	3
TELEPHOTO ZOOM	2	2
MACRO		
SHIFT		
SUPPORTS		
STANDARD TRIPOD		
POCKET TRIPOD		
CABLE RELEASE		
REMOTE TRIGGER		
CLOSE-UP		
SUPPLEMENTARY LENSES		
EXTENSION RINGS		
EXTENSION BELLOWS		
REVERSING RING		
SMALL REFLECTORS		
ACCESSORIES		
SPARE BATTERIES	1	1
TAPE		
TOOLS		
MARKER	1	1
NOTEBOOK	2	2
PLASTIC BAGS		
FILTERS		
UV	3	3
POLARIZING		
GRADUATED		
LIGHT-BALANCING	2	
COLOUR-COMPENSATING		2
FLUORESCENT	2	
FOR BLACK-AND-WHITE FILM		
SLOW		
MEDIUM	3	2
FAST	1	2
ULTRA-FAST	3	
DAYLIGHT	1	1
TYPE B	3	
LIGHTING		
ON-CAMERA FLASH	3	3
HIGH-OUTPUT PORTABLE		
MAINS FLASH		
SLAVE TRIGGER		
TUNGSTEN		
COLLAPSIBLE REFLECTOR		3
DIFFUSING SCREENS		
UMBRELLAS		
SPOTS		
STANDS		
CLAMPS		

C	D	E	F	G	H	I	J	K	L	M	N
2	2	2			2	2	2	3		2	
2	2	2			2	2	2	3		2	
2	2	2	2	2	2	2	2	2	2	2	2
2	2	2	2	2	2	2	2	2	2	2	2
			3	3	2	3					
2	2	3	2	2	2	2	3		2	2	2
2	3		2	2	2	2				2	2
3	2	2	3	3	2	2	1	3	2	1	3
3	3	2	2	2	1	1	1			3	3
	3	3	2	2	2	2					
			3	3	3	3					
1	2	2	3	3	1	1	1	1	1	3	3
		3	3		2	2		2	1		
3	3	2	3	3	2	2	2	3		3	
2	2	2	3	3	2	2	2	2	2	3	
					3	3					1
			1	1	3					3	
2	1		1	1	2	3			1	1	1
	3		3	2	3	1			3	2	1
3	2		1	1	2	2			2	1	1
									1		
										3	3
										2	1
											2
										3	2
										1	1
1	1	1	1	1	1	1	1	1	1	1	1
2	1			2			1		1	1	1
2	2			2			3		3	2	3
1	1	1	1	1	1	1	1	1	1	1	1
2	2	2	1	1	2	2	1	2	1	2	2
3					3	2	2	3	2		3
3	3	3	3		2	1	1	2	2	3	3
			3		2	2	2			3	
3			3	3	2	2					
2	1	3	3	1	3	3			3	2	2
3	2		3	2	3	3				3	3
	2		3	1							
2	3		1	1	1	1	2		3	1	2
2	1	2	2	2	1	1	1	2	1	1	1
3	3	1			3	3	3	2	2	3	3
		3						3	3		
1	2	2	1	1	1	1	1	1	1	2	2
	2	3	2	1						2	2
3	3	2						3	3	3	3
2	2			2					2	2	2
	2			2						2	2
3	3			3					2		
	2			2						2	2
2	2			2						2	
3	1			2						2	
2	1			3						3	
	3			3						2	3
1	1			1						1	2
1	2			1						1	1

Cleaning Make a habit of cleaning cameras and lenses regularly and often – at the very least, after a long trip. If you have to dismantle parts, such as the prism, do the cleaning in a clean, dry place. On location a blower brush, cloth, lens tissues and cotton buds will be enough equipment. In the studio, your kit might also include a compressed-air can, a stiff brush to clean the camera body, lens cleaning fluid, a mini-vacuum cleaner, wooden toothpicks, an eraser for battery contacts, and an anti-static gun.

For a thorough cleaning, follow this sequence:
- Strip down camera to easily removable parts (for example, detach lens, filter, back, batteries, etc.).
- Clean batteries and their contacts with eraser and cloth. Make sure no bits are left in the compartment.
- Remove outside dirt with stiff brush (and toothpick if necessary for crevices).
- Use compressed air or blower brush all over (but not compressed air on shutter curtain).
- Use anti-static gun on delicate parts such as lens surfaces and mirror.
- Clean crevices with cotton buds moistened with lens cleaning fluid.
- Wipe all non-delicate surfaces (guide rails, pressure plate, etc.) with soft lint-free cloth.
- Wipe lens surfaces with lens tissues (and lens cleaning fluid if necessary).
- Give a final quick burst of compressed air to remove any fresh dust.
- Use the anti-static gun just before re-assembling.

Protecting equipment When you are using the camera, avoid wherever possible getting it wet, dusty or hot. These are the three worst conditions for equipment. Water corrodes metal parts and shorts electrical circuits – salt water more rapidly than fresh – and although modern cameras use more plastic than metal, they are also more electronic than ever before. Light rain does no harm – just wipe the drops off quickly. Dust and sand are a danger because of what can happen later – the grains can work their way into the camera's mechanism and grind or jam moving parts. They can also scratch mirror, lens surfaces and film.

Heat is mostly a problem for film, but a black camera in direct sunlight, particularly in a locked car on a summer's day, can quickly become dangerously hot. This can weaken the lens cement, especially in older equipment, and can affect the electronics, apart from cooking whatever film may be inside. Keep everything in the shade when you are not using it. Cold weather in itself does little harm, but if you carry cold cameras into a heated room, they will get wet by condensation, just like the inside of a window pane. After cold-weather shooting, warm the camera up slowly – for instance, leave it in a colder part of the house for a while.

ACCIDENT PROCEDURES

Camera falls in fresh water
- Remove the film, but don't rewind it if it's wet. Open the camera back in complete darkness, remove the cassette and pull all of the film out as far as it will go. If it's only partly wet, hang to dry in the dark; if soaked, immerse in water in a light-tight container and process as soon as possible.
- Take off all easily-removable parts (lens, back, etc.) and dry as quickly as possible. A hair dryer is ideal, otherwise in the sun or on top of a radiator.
- Even if the camera still seems to work, have it checked professionally.

Camera falls in salt water
- As quickly as possible, immerse the camera in fresh water. Use a sealed container and fill it to the top so that there is no air.
- Either attempt drying it yourself (not likely to be successful without taking it to bits), or take it to a professional repair shop, still in the fresh water.

Dust or sand in camera
- Stop using the camera immediately. Otherwise, the grains are likely to work their way further in.
- Remove the film, ideally without rewinding (in complete darkness). Clean the lip of the cassette and rewind by hand, still in darkness.
- Strip down the camera and clean with compressed air and a soft brush.
- After cleaning, work all the moving parts. If you hear any grating or scratching, take it to a professional repair shop for cleaning.

Simple repairs Modern automated cameras are for the most part beyond DIY repair, being more electronic than mechanical. Basic manual-focus cameras offer slightly more possibilities, as do larger format cameras in which the parts are more accessible. Nevertheless, in an emergency, where the alternative is packing up and going home, it may be worth trying to keep the camera working. The danger is making things worse – and if the equipment is still under warranty, you will of course lose that.

If the camera stops working for inexplicable electronic reasons, check the batteries. Also check the controls carefully – you may have inadvertently pressed the wrong button. Mechanical damage is a different matter. Here the rule is that if you can see what's gone wrong, you have a chance of repairing it, even if only temporarily. If you drop a camera or lens, find the point of impact and investigate from there. Use pliers for bending back parts that have been knocked out of shape or alignment, epoxy resin (with great care!) to replace detached bits, and tape for a variety of repairs. Periodically check any parts of the camera that are held by screws – vibration and use can loosen them.

INDEX